WordPress SEO

How to SEO Your WordPress Site

By Dr. Andy Williams

ezSEONews.com
CreatingFatContent.com

Version 1.0
Released: 10th September 2013

Contents

Disclaimer and Terms of Use agreement

The author and publisher of this eBook and the accompanying materials have used their best efforts in preparing this eBook. The author and publisher make no representation or warranties with respect to the accuracy, applicability, fitness, or completeness of the contents of this eBook. The information contained in this eBook is strictly for educational purposes. Therefore, if you wish to apply ideas contained in this eBook, you are taking full responsibility for your actions.

The author and publisher disclaim any warranties (express or implied), merchantability, or fitness for any particular purpose. The author and publisher shall in no event be held liable to any party for any direct, indirect, punitive, special, incidental or other consequential damages arising directly or indirectly from any use of this material, which is provided "as is", and without warranties.

The author and publisher do not warrant the performance, effectiveness or applicability of any sites listed or linked to in this eBook.

All links are for information purposes only and are not warranted for content, accuracy or any other implied or explicit purpose.

The author and publisher of this book are not in any way associated with Google.

Introduction

Search Engine Optimization (SEO), is the process webmasters go through to encourage the search engines to rank their pages higher in the search results. Typically it involves working on the site itself. This is called on-site SEO, but it also involves working at site promotion, and that is what's known as off-site SEO.

Sites can be built in a number of different ways (PHP, HTML, Flash, etc.), using a wide variety of site-building tools, with common examples being Dreamweaver, Drupal, and WordPress, to name just three. Most websites and blogs share certain features that we can control, and use, to help with the on-site SEO. These features include things like the page title, headlines, body text, ALT tags and so on. In this respect, most sites can be treated in a similar manner when we consider on-site SEO. However, different platforms have their own quirks, and WordPress is no exception. Out-of-the-box WordPress doesn't do itself any SEO favours, and can in fact cause you ranking problems. This book will concentrate specifically for the on-page SEO of WordPress sites, highlighting the problems, and working through the numerous fixes.

By the end of this book, your WordPress site should be well optimized, without being 'over-optimized' (which is itself a contributing factor in Google penalties).

NOTE: This book assumes you are familiar with WordPress. If you are a complete beginner, I recommend you read my other book first, called 'WordPress for Beginners'. It's available on Amazon as either a Kindle book or physical book:

http://www.amazon.com/dp/B009ZVO3H6

1. The Biggest Sin - Duplicate Content

One of the main considerations when working on a WordPress site is duplicate content. For example, every post you create will also be posted on several other web pages within the site. Whether that post is shown in its entirety on all these pages, or as a shorter 'excerpt', is often controlled by the site's theme. Some themes will let you choose, whereas others will not.

So What Does This Mean to You, the SEO?

When a post is made on a WordPress, it may be published on all of the following web pages on that website, and at the same time:

1. Homepage
2. Post page. Every post is given its own web page.
3. Category page(s). Posts are assigned categories, and the category pages show all posts in that particular category.
4. Date archive page(s). These are pages that show all the posts made on a given date.
5. Tag page(s). Tag pages are another way of organizing your content. You can assign several words or phrases to each post, and for every word or phrase, a tag page is created. These tag pages show all posts that have been tagged with the specific word. Therefore if you used a tag 'blue widget' on five posts, the blue widget tag page will show all five posts.
6. Author page. This is an archive showing all of the posts made by a particular author.

That's six areas where the exact same post may show up!

If you assign just one category to a post, and one tag phrase, that means each post could appear on six web pages of the site **AT THE SAME TIME**. While I recommend you only assign a single post to just one category, tags are different. If you use tags, I'd recommend 3-5 per post. That would take the count up to nine or 10 pages showing identical content.

This type of duplication is bad (very bad!)

So the general rule that I recommend is to only include the 'full post' on ONE webpage of your site. On any other page where that post appears, you should be using excerpts, or in some cases just the title.

Having a high level of control is vital to removing this type of duplication, and the process begins by choosing a good template. The template should allow you to specify what you want posted on each of those six areas of potential duplication. I will therefore look at themes shortly, and explain what you need to look for when choosing a theme of your own.

First though, we should mention web hosting.

2. WordPress Web Hosting

OK, so you may be wondering why I am talking about web hosts. After all, isn't this supposed to be a book about WordPress SEO?

Yes, it is. However, the speed at which your site loads (and even the uptime of your site), are factors that are taken into account by search engines. Slow loading websites, or those which are unavailable for long periods of time (because the host server is down), suffer poorer rankings because of it. Sites which go down frequently, negatively impact the reputation you have with your visitors too.

There are many types of webhost, and lots of different plans that come with each one. You can get shared hosting, a managed or unmanaged Virtual Private Server (VPS), or a Dedicated Server. There are even some hosts that specialize in WordPress site hosting (although not all that advertise 'WordPress hosting' are setup specifically for it). I also know of one host that specializes in hosting WordPress sites that is built with the Genesis WordPress theme.

So which should you go for?

Well, that will depend on how much money you have available for your hosting. If you have a good budget, I would recommend going with a true 'WordPress optimized' web host. Here are two of the better known options:

1. WPEngine
2. WebSynthesis - This is hosting specifically designed for StudioPress themes (Genesis Framework), which we will look at in the next section of this book.

Links to both of these can be found on the book resource page here:

http://ezseonews.com/wpseo

If you visit those hosts, you'll notice that they are quite pricey, starting at $27/$29 per month for a single website. I have never used these personally, so cannot comment on their reliability. I do suggest you read the small print though, for whatever hosting package you decide to go with. The first host listed above has a price of $29 per month, but that only allows you 25,000 visitors a month in traffic. That is less than 850 visits a day, and for big, popular sites would be a problem.

2.1. Shared Hosting & Dedicated Servers

Most hosts offer a wide range of packages, from simple shared hosting, to dedicated servers (where you basically are given a computer and told to get on with it).

Dedicated servers, and unmanaged VPS hosting, both require a certain level of technical know-how, so I don't recommend you consider those unless you are technically capable.

For most people, shared hosting will be the best option because of the lower costs, especially for new sites. However, shared hosting is generally the most unreliable in terms of uptime and server response times (how long the server takes to respond to a request to show your web page).

As you look for a host, if you know of a website that is hosted with a particular company, I suggest you sign up for a free (or paid), account at Monitis.com and setup a 'monitor' to check the site every 5 minutes for response time. This will give you a good idea of how reliable that hosting company actually is.

See http://ezseonews.com/wpseo

Two of the most popular shared hosting companies are Hostgator and Bluehost. I have tried both, and until recently, Hostgator was the one I would have recommended. However, they have since 'upgraded' the server I was on, and uptime and response times plummeted as a result. Here is a screenshot from Monitis showing the details for one of my Hostgator hosted websites:

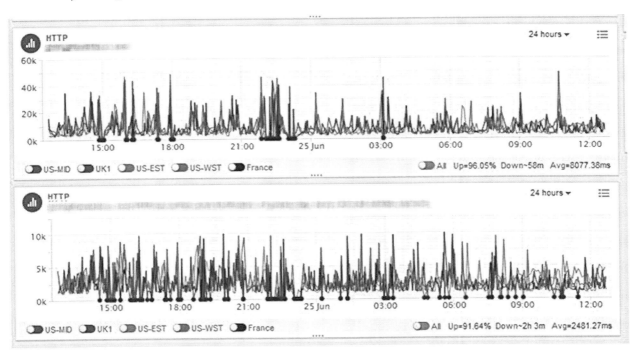

Look at all those peaks (these indicate when the server took longer to respond), and the small circular dots on the baseline (where the server did not respond).

The top graph is the homepage of the site. Over a 24 hour period, the homepage was down for 58 minutes, and the server response time was over eight seconds! That means it took eight seconds on average (although there are a lot of peaks over 40 seconds), to connect to my server, and that's even before the webpage started to download.

The lower graph is an internal page on the same site. This page gets less traffic so should have better response times - which it does - at around 2.5 seconds. However, that page was down for over two hours in the previous 24 hours.

I moved this site from Hostgator to Bluehost, but I found Bluehost to be just as unreliable. I guess Hostgator and Bluehost (being two of the most popular shared hosting companies); have suffered because of their own success.

I eventually found a host that I am happy with. They are called StableHost (http://ezseonews.com/stablehostreview).

StableHost offers free CDN with their hosting (which basically means your site is served from a network of servers around the globe). My site is hosted on their 'En-Basic' Enterprise hosting package, costing $19.95 per month at the time or writing. I have enabled CDN on the site (which only takes two minutes to setup), and here is the data from Monitis for the last 24 hours.

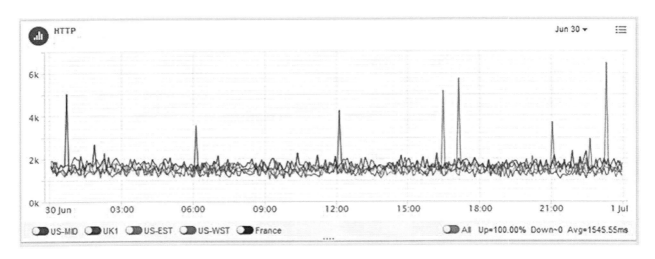

That's 100% uptime and a response time of around 1.5 seconds.

An inner page:

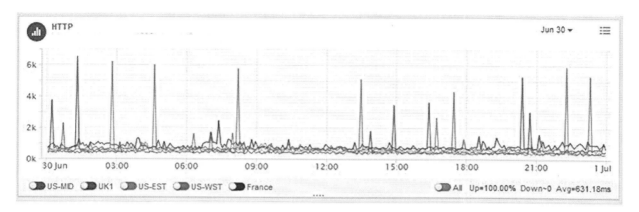

The inner page was down for one minute, and response time was 0.65 seconds.

You'll notice that there were far fewer peaks in response times on StableHost, and when there were peaks, it was a maximum of around 6 seconds, compared to the 40+ second peaks on Hostgator.

What all of this shows you, I hope, is that not all hosts are equal. If you want reliable hosting, go for the best that you can afford (and remember price does not necessarily correlate with quality). My order of choice would be:

1. WPEngine OR WebSynthesis.
2. Enterprise level hosting on StableHost, using CDN.
   http://ezseonews.com/stablehostreview
3. Shared hosting, but buyer-beware!

3. Themes & Theme Settings

There are lots of great themes out there, many of them are free. However, I don't generally recommend free themes, and here's why:

- They may not get updated.
- Some might include malicious code.
- A number of them contain footer links back to the creator's website (or any website they choose), which is really bad for SEO.
- They could be poorly written, and therefore slow to load.

There is one free theme that seems to have a huge following though, and is therefore updated regularly. It's called Atahualpa.

http://wordpress.org/themes/atahualpa

If you want to go down the free route, this is a good one to choose.

I have two recommended commercial themes for WordPress:

1. Genesis
2. Thesis
   Both of these can be found at http://ezseonews.com/wpseo

Both of these are 'frameworks'. Essentially a framework powers your WordPress site, and you change the appearance of your site by installing child themes, or skins that work with the framework.

Both Genesis and Thesis are excellent choices, though it has to be said that there is more of a learning curve with Thesis. For this reason, I recommend Genesis to my own students, and use it on *all* of my own sites. It's highly customizable, there are lots of child themes to choose from, and I can completely control the duplication issues that WordPress causes (see chapter one if you need to recap).

If you want to use a different theme, here is a five point checklist to help you decide:

1. Theme is fast loading.
2. Theme allows you to control how posts appear on all of the six 'potential duplication areas' of your site that we looked at earlier. You should have the options of full post, excerpt, or just the title.
3. Theme has at least one sidebar.
4. Theme allows one (or two) menus at the top of the website.
5. The theme does not include any mandatory links or attributions in the footer.

Points 2-5 can be answered by the theme's support desk. What about the first point though? How can you tell the load speed of a website, and check for potential problems with a template? You'll be pleased to know that this can be done quickly and simply.

For this we can use a free service at GTMetrix.com

GTMetrix allows you to analyse the page load times of any web page you want.

Find a site that uses the theme you are interested in using, and enter the URL of that site into GTMetrix. This tool then breaks down the page load speed into elements, and tells you exactly how long each element takes to load.

First the summary:

The summary gives you an A, B, or C rating of the page speed. You also get to see the page load time in seconds, the total page size, and the number of requests that were needed to download the page.

You should be looking for A or B ratings.

Under the main summary are 4 tabs: Page Speed, YSlow, Timeline, and History. The Page Speed and YSlow tabs offer advice on how to speed up the website. Click on any entry in these tables for an expanded view that shows you specifically what you need to do to fix an issue.

The timeline tab offers an interesting view of the page load speed. It tells you exactly how long each element on the page took to load. This is where you can get information on any 'theme-specific' problems.

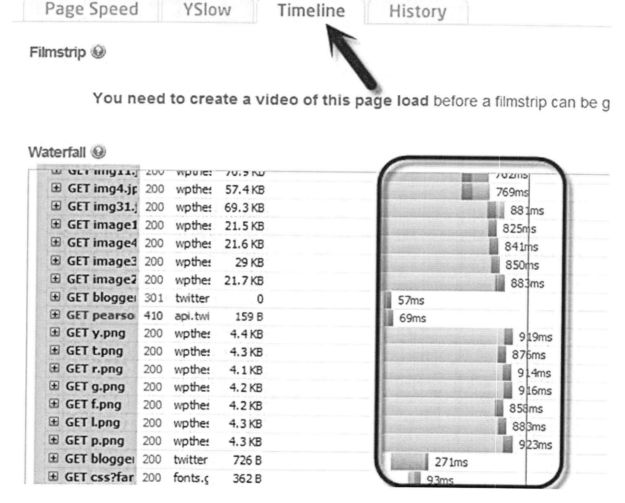

On the right hand side you can see the times taken to load each element. The timings are in milliseconds (1000ms equals one second).

On the left hand side you get a list of the page elements. If you move your mouse over an element, it will expand to show you the full URL of that component. For example, the element below took over half a second to load:

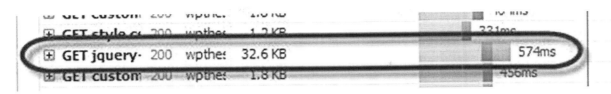

When I place my mouse over the element to check what it is, I see this:

In this case, it tells me that the element is related to the theme.

By looking for slow loading elements on the page, and checking whether they are related to the theme you want to use, you can make judgments on the how well that theme is optimized.

TIP: You will find that a lot of the slower loading elements on a page are images. Some images are related to the theme, whereas others are not – they are merely images added to a post. Don't worry about any slow loading image if it is not part of the theme.

Also, look for any element that has a large file size as these take longer to download. Here are a few in the theme I am testing:

The images of the demo theme are 1024 pixels by 485 pixels on their server. So the theme needs large images if you want to use its Slideshow feature. This means you will have physically large image files as well, although you could most probably reduce their size in KB using various techniques.

NOTE: If you use the Chrome Browser, you can install an extension called 'PageSpeed' (by Google). This will give you a measurement of how fast the site loads. Anything over 85 is considered a good score.

11

Here is the PageSpeed score for the same theme demo site shown in the GTMetrix example above:

Overview

The page Responsive Business Skin 2 got an overall Page Speed Score of 68 (out of 100). Learn more

Suggestion Summary

Click on the rule names to see suggestions for improvement.

- **Fast server response**
  (H)Improve server response time

- **Minimise payload**
  (H)Serve scaled images,(H)Optimise images,(L)Serve resources from a consistent URL,(L)Minify Ja
  (L)Minify CSS,(L)Minify HTML

One final thing to be mindful of is that it's unlikely the demo sites set up by theme vendors use caching plugins, or a content delivery network (CDN). That means the speeds you see with tools like this will probably be faster once it is setup on your server and properly optimized. With this in mind, don't concentrate too much on the page load times reported, and instead, look for large files that the theme uses, as these may cause speed problems on *any* server.

Hopefully you have seen that choosing a theme is not just as simple as finding one that looks good and using it. You need to make sure it will load fast too, and not contribute to longer loading times, especially if you go with cheaper, shared hosting.

For the rest of this book, I am going to be using the Genesis theme framework for most examples. If you haven't chosen a theme yet, or want my recommendation, go with the Genesis framework, and choose one of the child themes that you like.

If you are already using a different theme, don't worry, you can still follow along with all of the SEO advice given in this book.

3.1. Installing a Genesis Child Theme

This is a three step process:

1. Install the Genesis Framework.
2. Install the child theme.
3. Activate the **child theme**.

That's all there is to it.

The Genesis framework is needed by the child theme, so needs to remain installed on your server.

Once you have your child theme installed and activated, I recommend you **uninstall** all other themes that may be in your WordPress Dashboard. The reason for this is that old themes can often be routes taken by hackers to gain access to your site. We really don't want to give them that chance! So delete all themes (and plugins), that you are not using.

4. Google Tools

Google offer some great tools to webmaster, for free. I use them, and I recommend you do too. The three I am specifically referring to are Google Webmaster Tools, Google Analytics and Google authorship.

4.1 Google Webmaster Tools

Why should you use Google Webmaster Tools (GWT)?

Here are some good reasons:

- Get notified by Google if there is a problem with your site. Google will send you messages if, for example, your backlink profile looks spammy, or if your site is using an old version of WordPress, etc. They will also notify you if they detect malware on your website.
- Discover any HTML problems with your site. You can then follow the suggestions that GWT gives you to resolve the issue(s).
- Submit and check your sitemap (which can speed up indexing of your website).
- Select a geographic target audience. For example, if your website targets UK customers, but your site uses a .com extension, you can use GWT to tell Google that you want your site to be given more consideration in the UK.
- Check how well your site is being indexed by Google.
- Identify crawl errors. Google will tell you the URLs that it had trouble crawling, and the page which linked to that URL, thus allowing you to quickly identify and fix broken links on your site.
- Request Google removes specific URLs from their search results.
- Get a complete list of all links that point to your website (at least the ones that Google knows about). This can be very useful, especially in identifying links from spammy sites, which you can then disavow with the Google Disavow tool.
- Identify keywords that people are using to find your site. Google shows you the number of impressions in the search engines, how many clicks you got, the click through rate (CTR), and average position in the SERPs (Search Engine Results Pages). The CTR can be very useful for finding pages that may need their title/description tweaked so as to try and improve the CTR.

GWT offers a useful set of tools for all webmasters. I highly recommend you sign up and add your website(s) to your account, so you can track them all.

Sign up here: http://bit.ly/oGe6PP

4.2 Google Analytics

Google Analytics is a free visitor tracking tool, which is far more powerful than many commercial tools that are available.

Reasons to use Google Analytics (GA) include:

- See details of your visitors, like the search term they used to find your site, how long they spent on your site, which browser they use, what country they come from, and so on.
- Get real time statistics, showing how many people are on your site right now, and which pages they are viewing, etc.
- Connect your Google Analytics account to your GWT account, and Google AdSense account, for even more tracking features.
- Split-test different versions of, for example, a sales page.
- Set up custom alerts, to notify you about the things that are important to your business.
- Monitor mobile traffic.
- Lots of other features...

Sign up here: http://www.google.com/analytics/

Once you have signed up for Google Analytics and registered your site with them, you'll be given some tracking code to insert into your website. Whichever theme you use, you should have an easy way to insert your analytics code. Here is a screenshot for the Genesis theme (**Genesis -> Theme Settings** menu):

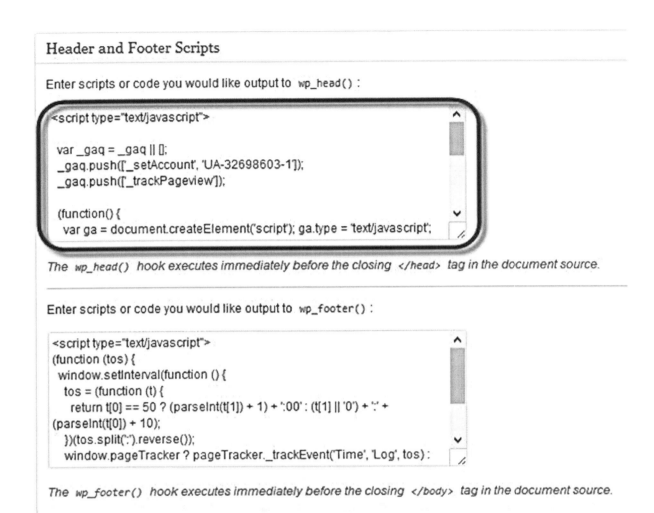

Header and Footer Scripts

Enter scripts or code you would like output to wp_head() :

```
<script type="text/javascript">

var _gaq = _gaq || [];
_gaq.push(['_setAccount', 'UA-32698603-1']);
_gaq.push(['_trackPageview']);

(function() {
  var ga = document.createElement('script'); ga.type = 'text/javascript';
```

The wp_head() hook executes immediately before the closing </head> tag in the document source.

Enter scripts or code you would like output to wp_footer() :

```
<script type="text/javascript">
(function (tos) {
  window.setInterval(function () {
    tos = (function (t) {
      return t[0] == 50 ? (parseInt(t[1]) + 1) + ':00' : (t[1] || '0') + ':' +
(parseInt(t[0]) + 10);
    })(tos.split(':').reverse());
    window.pageTracker ? pageTracker._trackEvent('Time', 'Log', tos) :
```

The wp_footer() hook executes immediately before the closing </body> tag in the document source.

If possible, insert the analytics code into the wp_head() section of your website.

There are some known issues with Google Analytics and the way it reports 'time on site' and 'bounce rate'. For that reason, I have also inserted another script into the wp_footer() area of my theme (see screenshot above). You can read more about these issues, and grab the code yourself here:

http://bit.ly/KbUvs9

4.3 Google Authorship

Google authorship is not so much a tool, as something you setup between your website and your Google plus profile. By linking your website content to your Google Plus profile, you get these three benefits:

1. Tell Google that you are the author of the content. If someone then steals your work and reposts it on another site, Google knows that you were the true, original author.
2. You can have your Gravatar image (globally recognized avatar), show up next to your content in the search results, which in turn can add social proof to your listing, and increase click through rates (CTR).
3. Build Author Rank. This is thought to be an increasingly important ranking factor. The more Google trust an author, the higher they will rank that author's work.

We will revisit Google authorship later in the book, and I'll show you how to set it up so that the posts on your site (and on guest blogs), are assigned to you.

5. Screen Options

The WordPress Dashboard has some settings hidden away in the top right corner of its screen. You should see the link to **Screen Options**, and they control what you see on the screen when you are moving around the dashboard. The screen options are a series of checkboxes which you can check or uncheck depending on what you want displayed.

These screen options change depending on where you are in the dashboard. For example, if you are editing a post, the screen options will be specific to that task:

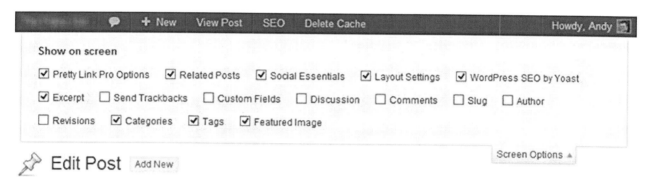

If there is something you do not use, you can uncheck it and it disappears from your dashboard, helping to reduce any unnecessary clutter.

As another example, here are the screen options when editing the settings of the YARPP WordPress plugin (which we will look at later):

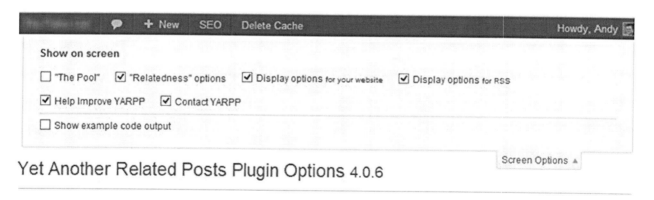

If you are ever looking for something mentioned in this book, or any other, but don't see it in your dashboard, then check the screen options. There's a good chance you have that particular box unchecked.

6. WordPress Settings Menu

During the initial setup of a WordPress site, it's a good idea to go through the Settings menu first to make sure everything is set up properly. You will find this settings menu in the left sidebar of your Dashboard. Mouse-over the word 'Settings' and a popup menu will appear displaying the options. Click on the word 'Settings' and that menu integrates into the sidebar, below the main Settings heading:

Once we install a few plugins later on, there will be more items in the Settings menu, but we'll deal with those as and when we get to them.

Note that I will only be covering the settings that are specifically related to good SEO.

6.1. General Settings

Site Title & Tagline

The top two items in the General settings are Site Title and Tagline. Later in the book we will look at creating a custom logo image and using that on the website, but until you create & upload that image, the Site Title and Tagline entered here will be displayed at the top of every page on your site.

DO NOT stuff keywords into the site name or tagline fields. Your site name will most probably be based on your domain name, and the tagline should be a short sentence specifying your site's goal, philosophy or slogan.

There is a good article on creating a tagline on the Copyblogger website:

http://www.copyblogger.com/create-a-tagline/

If you need help with yours, I suggest you read that.

E-mail Address

The only other setting we need to concern ourselves with on this page is the email address. This will be used by WordPress, plugins, and a free external service (Gravatar.com). We'll be looking at these later, so your email address needs to be correct.

6.2. Writing Settings

In terms of SEO, the only setting we need to change here is the **Update Services**. These are a list of web services that get notified whenever new content gets published on the site. Having a good 'ping list' will help your content get indexed quicker too.

Search Google for "WordPress ping list" and you'll find a list of sites to include. Simply copy and paste the list into the Update Services box, and then save your settings.

Update Services

When you publish a new post, WordPress automatically notifies th the Codex. Separate multiple service URLs with line breaks.

```
http://api.my.yahoo.com/rss/ping
http://1470.net/api/ping
http://api.feedster.com/ping
http://api.moreover.com/ping
http://api.moreover.com/RPC2
http://api.my.yahoo.com/RPC2
http://bblog.com/ping.php
```

Save Changes

6.3. Reading Settings

Latest posts vs. static page

At the top of the Reading Settings is the **Front page displays:**

This will tell WordPress which if the two options to use for the homepage on your site. You can select:

1. **Your latest posts**
2. **A static page**

If you want to have a static page as your homepage, i.e., an article that does not change, you can create that article as a WordPress 'Page', and then select that page here to use as the homepage (front page).

In this book, we will be using a Genesis theme, and the home pages in Genesis are widgetized. If you're not sure what that means, don't worry. Just realise that it's good, and we'll look into it later in the Homepage section of this book. To take advantage of this fantastic Genesis homepage feature, you need to leave the settings here to show 'Your latest posts' on the front page (which is the default setting).

Next up on the Reading Settings is deciding how many posts to display on the homepage and archive pages (like category page, author page, etc), and decide what information is shown in RSS feeds (something WordPress generates for your site).

Blog pages show at most	10 [⬍] posts
Syndication feeds show the most recent	10 [⬍] items
For each article in a feed, show	⦿ Full text ○ Summary
Search Engine Visibility	☐ Discourage search engines from indexing this site *It is up to search engines to honor this request.*

The default setting is 10, which means WordPress will show 10 posts on the homepage, 10 on the category pages, and 10 on the author page, etc. If there are more than 10 posts to show, then the remainder will be added, in batches of 10, to additional pages, and you'll get a next/previous type navigation to move between them.

I would recommend you leave the '**Blog pages show at most**' set to 10.

Beneath that is the '**Syndication feeds show the most recent**' option.

WordPress creates RSS feeds for your site (see my WordPress for Beginners book if you want to read more on this - http://www.amazon.com/dp/B009ZVO3H6). Your site will have a main feed, plus there will be feeds for category pages, tag pages, and so on. This setting tells WordPress how many items to include in the feed. With Google's Penguin algorithm looking at the over-optimization of inbound links, I'd limit the RSS feed to a maximum of 10. In the past, webmasters have included 100 items (or more), and that would mean any site that is displaying your RSS feed will contain 100 links back to it. Before Google Penguin, that was OK, but not now. So I would suggest leaving this number set at 10.

You now have to decide what the feed contains, i.e., all the content of your posts, or just a summary of them. Select '**Summary**' because otherwise you are making if far too easy for scraper software tools to copy (steal), your content. These software tools monitor RSS feeds and strip the content out. Your content is then likely to be posted on one or more spammy sites around the internet, and that's not good.

Later in this book we will look at Google Authorship, and one reason I recommend you use this is to tell Google that you are the author of the content. Essentially, when it's set up, any new posts you add to your site will automatically be tagged in Google with you as the author. Then if someone does steal your work, Google knows who the real author/owner is, and rewards you in its search results pages.

The final option on this page is 'Search Engine Visibility'. When some people develop a website, they want it to be finished before the search engines come to spider the site. This option allows you to do just that. By checking the box, your website will basically tell the search engines to ignore it until you decide the time is right, and uncheck this option.

I recommend you leave this box unchecked from the start, that's unless you have good reason to not want the content indexed as you create it. As I add content to a website, I *want* Google to find and index it as soon as possible. If they see new content being added over a short period of time, they'll know the site is under construction and needs to be spidered more regularly so as to keep their index up to date. By leaving this option unchecked, you are encouraging the search engine spiders to crawl your site, and that's a good thing.

6.4 Discussion Settings

The Discussion Settings refer to the commenting system built into WordPress.

Google likes to see visitor interaction on a website, so this is an important part of your WordPress SEO, and so you'll want to keep the comments enabled.

At the top of these settings, you will see:

Default article settings

☑ Attempt to notify any blogs linked to from the article
☑ Allow link notifications from other blogs (pingbacks and trackbacks)
☑ Allow people to post comments on new articles
(These settings may be overridden for individual articles.)

These boxes should all be left checked.

The first option means WordPress will try to send a notification to any blog you link to in your posts. This lets a site owner know you have linked to them, and can sometimes result in a link back.

The second option is the first one in reverse. If someone links to your site, then WordPress will notify you so that you can see who's linking to you. This has been abused by spammers and you will get a lot of false positives here, but you'll still get these even if you disable this option.

The final option simply tells WordPress to allow visitors to comment on your posts. This is what we want – visitor participation.

The '**Other comment settings**' section has a few more options:

☑ Comment author must fill out name and e-mail

☐ Users must be registered and logged in to comment

☐ Automatically close comments on articles older than 14 ⬍ days

☑ Enable threaded (nested) comments 5 ⌄ levels deep

☐ Break comments into pages with 50 ⬍ top level comments per page and the last ⌄ page displayed by default

Comments should be displayed with the older ⌄ comments at the top of each page

Check the first box so that anyone leaving a comment must enter a name and an email address.

The second box should be unchecked unless you are creating some kind of membership site where people need to register in order to participate.

Leave the third box unchecked too, unless there is a reason why you want to close comments on older posts. I personally like to keep comments open indefinitely, and if there is a post where I want to close them, I can do that in the 'Edit Post' screen, just for that one post.

The fourth checkbox will enable nested comments. This is something that not only makes the comments look better, but more intuitive for your visitors. This is because replies to a specific comment will be nested under the original, and this in turn makes following the conversation much easier.

The next option allows you to spread comments across pages once you get over a certain number of remarks on the main post page. This is a good idea if your site gets a lot of comments, because the more you have, the longer the page will take to load.

If you anticipate a lot of comments, enable this option. You can also specify here whether you want comments to be shown with the oldest or newest first. I personally think it makes more sense to have older comments at the top. That way, the comments are chronological, but this is a personal preference.

Next on this page is the 'E-mail me whenever' settings. Do you want to be notified when someone comments on a post? If so, make sure that option is checked. I recommend you check this so that you get instant notifications of any new comments posted on your site. This means you get to reply quickly. Fast responses to comments are important, and it makes the visitor feel that you care. Practising good interaction means there's a much better chance the commenter will come back and visit your site again.

The second email option is to notify you when a comment is held for moderation. You can uncheck this, because in a moment we will tell WordPress to hold ALL comments for moderation, and we are already getting notified every time someone posts a comment anyway.

In the 'Before a comment appears' section, check the first box, and uncheck the second.

Before a comment appears   ☑ An administrator must always approve the comment
                              ☐ Comment author must have a previously approved comment

This will force ALL comments to appear in a moderation queue, and will only go live on your site once you approve them.

This means the next couple of settings in the 'Comment Moderation' section are irrelevant, since ALL comments are now held for moderation. We can therefore ignore that section.

NOTE: Moderating comments might sound like a lot of work, but it is essential. If you have your site set up to auto-approve comments, you pages will end up full of spam remarks, and all kinds of gobbledegook. Needless to say that would take a lot more time cleaning up than moderating comments.

The 'Comment Blacklist' is a good way to fight spam. You can include email addresses, IP addresses, and certain words in the box. If a comment matches any of those lines, it is automatically marked as spam. If I end up getting a lot of spam comments from a particular IP address, I usually add that to this list as well.

Comment Blacklist

When a comment contains any of these words in its ⟨
"press" will match "WordPress".

```
198.50.159.185
188.143.232.31
188.165.197.19
46.165.225.214
220.200.23.103
zyban
zolus
zithromax
zenegra
z411
```

You can also search Google for a "WordPress comment blacklist" which will get you started. Just add one item per line, and save your changes when done.

The final section on the Discussion Settings relates to the use of "Avatars".

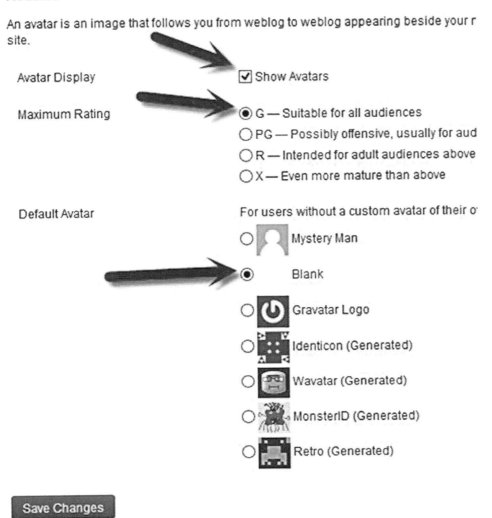

Avatars

An avatar is an image that follows you from weblog to weblog appearing beside your r site.

Avatar Display   ☑ Show Avatars

Maximum Rating   ⦿ G — Suitable for all audiences
                         ○ PG — Possibly offensive, usually for aud
                         ○ R — Intended for adult audiences above
                         ○ X — Even more mature than above

Default Avatar   For users without a custom avatar of their o

                         ○ Mystery Man

                         ⦿ Blank

                         ○ Gravatar Logo

                         ○ Identicon (Generated)

                         ○ Wavatar (Generated)

                         ○ MonsterID (Generated)

                         ○ Retro (Generated)

[Save Changes]

An Avatar is a small image of the author. If the author of a comment has a Gravatar (http://gravatar.com/) assigned to the email address, and they use that same email to leave a comment, then that Gravatar is shown as their avatar.

I recommend you check '**Show Avatars**'. I think this helps the comment section become more active, since visitors to your site can see little photos of real people leaving remarks. Site visitors like to know who they are dealing with, a face behind the name as it were, so these images help instil confidence and help gain site credibility.

I would recommend you check the 'G' rating, so the avatars on your site should be suitable viewing for all ages.

27

Also, select 'Blank' for the default avatar. Avatars take time to load, thus increasing the page load time. With blank selected, if a person does not have a Gravatar setup, no image is loaded for that person.

6.5. Media Settings

While the settings here allow us to determine the maximum sizes of images in posts, I recommend you do that manually on a post by post basis at the time you create them. Therefore, there are no specific settings in the Media Settings section that we need to change for SEO purposes.

6.6 Permalinks Settings

The Permalink settings are important, because whatever you enter here will influence the way the URLs are displayed for the pages on your website.

The default WordPress setting will produce URLs like this:

Mydomain.com/?p=123

The '?p=123' parameter in this URL is simply a call for the page with Page ID = 123. This is not very useful for visitors, it looks ugly, and it's certainly not helpful to search engines.

A lot of people will use the 'post name' option, which uses the post title in the URL. Actually it uses the post 'slug' which is the portion of the URL that represents the post. But by default that will be the post title unless you change it. For example, if you had a post called 'Liverpool win in Istanbul', then the URL for that post would look like this:

Mydomain.com/Liverpool-win-in-istanbul

Note that capitals are stripped out, as well as some other characters like apostrophes.

There is a problem that I read about with this permalink structure. Basically, as the site gets larger, WordPress struggles to locate the post if it only has the post 'slug' (filename), to go on. It therefore takes longer to load pages. In order to fix this problem, you need to add in either the page ID, or the category into the permalink. I actually recommend you use a permalink that contains the category anyway, so even if this wasn't an issue with the latest WordPress, I'd still recommend you choose 'Custom Structure' and enter the following as your permalink structure:

28

/%category%/%postname%/

Here it is in my settings:

○ Custom Structure   http://████████.com /%category%/%postname%/

Now the URL of any page will include the category and filename of the post. A typical URL for a post might look like this:

Mydomain.com/dog-breeds/alsatians

So in this case, the post filename is 'Alsatians', and the post is in the 'dog breeds' category.

IMPORTANT:

With Google's Panda and Penguin looking for what Google calls 'webspam', we need to be very careful about choosing the correct category names for our site, especially if we are including the category in the URL.

For example, if your site is called mydietreviews.com, and you had a category called 'diets', then a URL might look like this:

my**diet**reviews.com/**diets**/hollywood-**diet**/

This URL has the word 'diet' in it three times. That could well be seen as keyword stuffing and should be avoided. If you think that this type of situation will arise on your site with the categories you have chosen, then play it safe and use this alternative permalink:

/%post_id%/%postname%/

Post_id is replaced with the ID of the post (basically an integer number that is assigned to a post at the time you publish it). Your URL may then look like:

my**diet**reviews.com/1045/hollywood-**diet**/

A URL like this appears is a little less spammy, yet includes the page_id which helps WordPress locate the page faster.

At the bottom of the common settings, there are some optional choices:

Optional

If you like, you may enter custom structures for your category and tag URLs here. For example, using topics as your category base would make your category links like http://example.org/topics/uncategorized/ . If you leave these blank the defaults will be used.

Category base	
Tag base	

Save Changes

To understand what these options do, I need to tell you how WordPress assigns the URL for category pages and tag pages. Essentially, every category page will have the word 'category' in the URL, and every tag page will have the word 'tag' in the URL. Therefore, using the examples above, the category page URL would look like this:

mydietreviews.com/**category**/diets/

This category page will then show all the posts in the diets category.

Similarly, a tag page URL would look something like this:

mydietreviews.com/tag/fat-loss/

Any posts on your site that were tagged with the term 'fat loss' would be listed on this page.

OK, back to category base and tag base settings. These will replace the word 'category' or 'tag' in these URLs, with whatever you specify here.

If you set the category base to be 'abracadabra', then the category URL would become:

mydietreviews.com/**abracadabra**/diets/

Before Panda and Penguin, category and tag bases were used to keyword stuff the URLs. Today, leave them blank as they will only get your site into trouble.

7. Plugins

Before we look at the plugins, I need to mention that many are updated frequently and their appearance can change a little as a consequence. That means the screenshots in this book may not be identical to what you are seeing in your Dashboard. Most changes are minor though, so you should still be able to set everything up properly, even if your plugin is a different version to the one that I am showing in this book.

What I am going to do in this section is get you to install certain plugins. We won't go through the configuration of each one just yet; we'll do that later in the book when we need to achieve certain SEO goals.

There are a few essential plugins to get your WordPress site ready for the search engines. I'll cover these first, and I recommend you install ALL three of them. I'll then list a few other plugins that you may find useful, and explain what they do. You can hold off installing these until you know whether you will need them or not.

To install the plugins, login to the Dashboard, and from the left side column, go to Plugins -> Add New. You will see a search box & button. Enter the plugin names in the search box as I state them below, and then install and activate each one.

7.1. Essential Plugins

1. WordPress SEO

This is a comprehensive SEO plugin that will create a self-updating sitemap and allow us fine control over the SEO of the site.

Search for "WordPress SEO".

This is the one you are looking for, by Joost de Valk:

WordPress SEO 1.4.13 by Yoast ☆☆☆☆☆	WordPress out of the box is already technically quite a good platform for SEO, this was true when I wrote my original WordPress SEO article in 2008 and it's still true today, but that doesn't mean you can't improve it further! This plugin is written from the ground up by WordPress SEO consultant and WordPress developer Joost de Valk to improve your site's SEO on all needed aspects. While this Word... By Joost de Valk.
Details | Install Now	

Click the Install now link, and once installed, activate the plugin.

2. W3 Total Cache

This plugin is essential because it speeds up your website. Page load speed, as mentioned previously, is an important part of SEO. Google like fast loading pages, and once we have this plugin configured, your site should load several times faster than before.

Search for "W3 Total Cache".

This is the one you are looking for, by Frederick Townes:

| W3 Total Cache 0.9.2.11 Details \| Install Now | ☆☆☆☆☆ | The only WordPress Performance Optimization (WPO) framework; designed to improve user experience and page speed. Recommended by web hosts like: Page.ly, Synthesis, DreamHost, MediaTemple, Go Daddy, Host Gator and countless more. Trusted by countless companies like: AT&T, stevesouders.com, mattcutts.com, mashable.com, smashingmagazine.com, makeuseof.com, yoast.com, kiss925.com, pearsonified.c... By Frederick Townes. |

Install and activate the plugin.

3. Dynamic Widgets

The final essential plugin is called Dynamic Widgets, and this allows us to create dynamic, context-sensitive sidebars (and other elements), on our web site.

Search for "dynamic widgets", and look for this one by Qurl:

| Dynamic Widgets 1.5.4 Details \| Installed | ☆☆☆☆☆ | Dynamic Widgets gives you full control on which pages your widgets will appear. It lets you dynamically show or hide widgets on WordPress pages by setting conditional logic rules with just a few mouse clicks. No knowledge of PHP required. No fiddling around with conditional tags. You can set conditional rules by Role, Dates, Browser, Theme Template, Language (WPML or QTranslate), URL, for the Home... By Qurl. |

Install and activate the plugin.

That's it. Those are the three essential plugins we need to setup for SEO purposes.

7.2 Non-essential Plugins

I won't be going into details on installing and configuring these plugins. I will just tell you what they do, and if you want to add them to your site, you can use the help documents that come with them should you need assistance setting them up.

Remember this though; the more plugins you install on your site, the slower it will potentially load. Therefore keep plugins to a minimum, and only use ones that you actually need.

1. WP Policies

This plugin will create a default set of 'legal' documents for your site. Things like disclaimers, terms of service, privacy page, etc. I am no lawyer, so cannot comment on how good these documents are, but they are the types of documents you need to have on your site, so I think they're better than having none.

Search for "wp policies"

| WP Policies | 1.0 | ☆☆☆☆☆ | WP Policies allows you to quickly add pre-written privacy policy and disclaimer statements to your Wordpress blog. |
| Details \| Install Now | | | The plugin currently comes with 10 policies that you can edit depending on your blog. By Offline Marketing Tools. |

2. Google XML Sitemaps for Video

If you have a lot of videos on your site, even YouTube videos, then this plugin will create a separate sitemap for them that you can submit to Google Webmaster Tools; hopefully getting better indexing rates for them. As a bonus, Google likes to rank video highly in its search engine results pages (SERPs), especially YouTube, so if you have YouTube videos embed into your pages, you can get them indexed with this plugin.

Search for "video sitemap"

Google XML Sitemap for Videos	2.6.1	★★★★☆	Sitemaps are a way to tell Google, Bing and other search engines about web pages, images and video content on your site that they may otherwise not discover. The Video Sitemap plugin will generate an XML Sitemap for your WordPress blog using all YouTube videos that you may have embedded in your blog posts. Your Video Sitemap will includes web pages which embed videos from YouTube or which links ... By Amit Agarwal.
Details | Install Now			

3. YARPP

This one stands for 'Yet Another Related Posts Plugin'. It basically creates a list of related posts, dynamically, for each post on your site. These posts can be automatically inserted after a post's content, or you can insert related posts as a widget, meaning you can place them into any widgetized area of your template, for example, a sidebar.

Search for "yet another related post"

Yet Another Related Posts Plugin	4.0.6	★★★★☆	Yet Another Related Posts Plugin (YARPP) gives you a list of posts and/or pages related to the current entry, introducing the reader to other relevant content on your site. Thumbnails: a beautiful new thumbnail display, for themes which use post thumbnails (featured images) New in YARPP 4! Related posts, pages, and custom post types: Learn about CPT support. Templating: The YARPP templating syst... By mitcho (Michael Yoshitaka Erlewine).
Details | Install Now			

4. Contact form 7

This plugin makes it easy to setup a contact form on your site. A contact form is an essential part of any website. Whether or not you expect your visitors to contact you, the search engines expect good sites to have this option.

Search for "contact form 7"

Contact Form 7	3.4.2	☆☆☆☆☆	Contact Form 7 can manage multiple contact forms, plus you can customize the form and the mail contents flexibly with simple markup. The form supports Ajax-powered submitting, CAPTCHA, Akismet spam filtering and so on. Docs & Support You can find docs, FAQ and more detailed information about Contact Form 7 on contactform7.com. If you were unable to find the answer to your question on the FAQ... By Takayuki Miyoshi.
Details | Install Now			

5. WP-DBManager

This plugin is one I install on all of my sites. It looks after your WordPress database, optimizing it regularly, and sends you periodic backups via email (crucial in case you ever have a server crash, or your site gets hacked).

Search for "WP DB Manager"

WP-DBManager	2.63	☆☆☆☆☆	Allows you to optimize database, repair database, backup database, restore database, delete backup database , drop/empty tables and run selected queries. Supports automatic scheduling of backing up, optimizing and repairing of database. Previous Versions WP-DBManager 2.40 For WordPress 2.7.x WP-DBManager 2.31 For WordPress 2.1.x To 2.6.x WP-DBManager 2.05 For WordPress 2.0.x WP-DBManager 1.00 F... By Lester 'GaMerZ' Chan.
Details | Install Now			

6. Automatic Updater

Keeping your WordPress install (and plugins), up to date is a good idea to prevent security holes in your site. This plugin will do just that, checking for updates periodically and then automatically updating WordPress and/or your plugins. I personally use this, but only have it set to update WordPress, not the plugins. Plugins can take a while to catch up once a new version of WordPress is released, so I prefer to manually update those once the authors tell us they are compatible. Later in the book, I'll show you how to manually update WordPress and the plugins.

Search for "automatic updater"

Automatic Updater Details | Install Now	0.8.5	⭐⭐⭐⭐⭐	Automatic Updater keeps your WordPress install up to date with the latest releases automatically, as soon as the update is available. It supports updating stable releases, nightly releases, or even regular SVN checkouts! If you're working on a WordPress Multisite install, it will properly restrict the options page to your Network Admin. While this will be useful for the vast majority of sites, p... By pento.

7. Broken Link Checker

If your site has a lot out outbound links to other websites (by the way, linking to authority sites within your niche is a good idea), then this plugin can check your outbound links and tell you if any are broken. Google don't like broken links on a site, and may punish you if you have a lot of them. Therefore, this plugin can help ensure this does not become a problem.

Search for "broken link checker"

Broken Link Checker Details | Install Now	1.8	⭐⭐⭐⭐☆	This plugin will monitor your blog looking for broken links and let you know if any are found. Features Monitors links in your posts, pages, comments, the blogroll, and custom fields (optional). Detects links that don't work, missing images and redirects. Notifies you either via the Dashboard or by email. Makes broken links display differently in posts (optional). Prevents search engines from f... By Janis Elsts.

8. Social Essentials

Social Essentials adds social media sharing to your site. That is, buttons for your visitors to share your content on Twitter, Facebook, Google +, Pinterest, and Stumbleupon. It is a great idea to add this feature to your site, as Google are taking notice of social signals and using them in their ranking algorithm. Encourage your visitors to share your content!

To be honest, there are a lot of plugins with similar functionality, so if you already know of one that you like, use it instead of social essentials.

Search for "social essentials"

Social Essentials - Social Stats and Sharing Buttons	1.3.1	☆☆☆☆☆	Social Essentials provides you with: A simple way to add social sharing buttons to your posts and pages. A simple way to add a call-to action to your buttons, to increase social engagement. Stats that show you how much your content is being shared, in detail. The following social networks are supported for both stats and buttons: Twitter Facebook (like/share button) Google+ StumbleUpon Pinte... By Shane Melaugh.
Details	Install Now			

9. Growmap or Akismet

These are two anti-comment spam plugins, i.e., they block spam in comments automatically. Install either of these and you'll get far fewer spam comments. Of the two, Akismet (which comes pre-installed with WordPress), is the better option in my opinion, however, it is also commercial. Growmap is a free alternative.

Search for "Growmap"

Growmap Anti Spambot Plugin	1.2	☆☆☆☆☆	This plugin will add a client side generated checkbox to your comment form asking users to confirm that they are not a spammer. It is a lot less trouble to click a box than it is to enter a captcha and because the box is genereated via client side javascript that bots cannot see, it should stop 99% of all automated spam bots. A check is made that the checkbox has been checked before the comment i... By Andy Bailey.
Details	Install Now			

10. Pretty Link

Pretty Link Lite is a free plugin (there is a commercial version too, but the free version is all most people need). What this plugin does, is allow you to setup redirects on your site. Therefore, if you want to use an affiliate link on your page(s), you could set up a link like mydomain.com/affproduct, and this would redirect to the affiliate site. Why bother? If you don't know why you would want to do this, then you most probably don't need this plugin. One other nice feature of it though, is that it tracks clicks on all of the pretty links you set up, which can be very useful.

Search for "pretty link lite"

37

Pretty Link Lite 1.6.4	☆☆☆☆☆	Pretty Link Pro Upgrade to Pretty Link Pro Pretty Link Pro is a significant upgrade to Pretty Link Lite that adds many tools and redirection types that will allow you to create pretty links automatically, cloak links, auto-tweet links, replace keywords thoughout your blog with pretty links and much more. You can learn more about Pretty Link Pro here: About | Features | Pricing Prett... By Caseproof.
Details | Install Now		

11. Social Stickers

Social Stickers is a neat way of adding social follow buttons to your site. Do you want your visitors to follow you on Twitter? Facebook? Google +? Pinterst? Quora? Social Stickers will add these buttons to your site.

Search for "social stickers"

Social Stickers 2.1	☆☆☆☆☆	This is a simple plugin that shows the various social networks you use in the form of "stickers" (see screenshots). It is also fully themable and you can make your own theme in a minute. What this plugin offers: Themes (fully themable, you can easily create your own theme) You can customize the order of the icons (each theme has its own order) Add your own social networks Widget mode Supports s... By Bostjan Cigan.
Details | Install Now		

Finally there are a few commercial plugins that might interest you. One in particular helps with on-site SEO.

12. CI Backlinks

This plugin allows you automate the internal linking of content across your site. It is a plugin I use on all of my websites, because internal linking done manually is an almost impossible task. For example, when you add a new post to your website, you'd need to go and find all other posts that mention that topic so an internal link can be created. With this plugin, you setup the rules and internal links are updated automatically as you add new content.

More details from: http://ezseonews.com/wpseo

13. VIA Curation

Getting you visitors to contribute content to your site is a great idea as it gets people involved with your project. VIA Curation does this by way of submission forms. From these forms, your visitors can submit articles, images and videos to your website. Obviously you get to moderate all submissions.

More details from: http://ezseonews.com/wpseo

14. WP Secure

This plugin helps to keep your WordPress install secure against hackers. When this plugin is installed, even if a hacker gets hold of your username and password, they'll still not be able to login. How's that possible? It's magic! No, not really, but it is clever!

More details from: http://ezseonews.com/wpseo

15. WP Sticky

The next plugin is WP Sticky. It allows us to 'stick' posts at the top of archive pages:

| WP-Sticky

Details \|
Install Now | 1.50 | ☆ ☆ ☆ ☆ ☆ | Modified from Adhesive by Owen Winkler.
All the information (general, changelog, installation, upgrade, usage) you need about this plugin can be found here: WP-Sticky Readme.
It is the exact same readme.html is included in the zip package. By Lester 'GaMerZ' Chan. |

This comes in handy for non-Genesis themes if you want to create introductions to category and tag pages (see later in the book for details on this).

OK, that brings an end to my list of essential, and not so essential, plugins. Make sure you get the essentials installed before moving on. We'll be starting to configure them very soon.

8. Keeping WordPress Up to Date - WordPress & Plugins

It is important that you always keep WordPress and plugins up to date. Hackers typically look for exploits in WordPress, so updates fix any known problems, thus keeping your website protected.

Fortunately, WordPress makes it easy to know if there are any updates to the core program itself, or any plugins and themes that you have installed.

If a WordPress update is available, you'll see the notification in the Dashboard at the top & center.

WordPress 3.5.2 is available! Please update now.

Genesis 1.8.2 is available. Check out what's new or update now.

As you can see from the screenshot, some themes, like Genesis, also show its update notifications at the top of the Dashboard too, directly under the WordPress announcement.

To update WordPress, you can just click the '**Please update now**' link and follow the simple instructions.

There are other visual cues in the dashboard that also notify you of various updates.

If a plugin update is available, you'll see a number appear next to Plugins in the left sidebar. The number tells you how many plugin updates are available.

Finally, there is a quick way to see all updates in one area of the Dashboard. Click on the word 'Dashboard', at the top of the left sidebar, and the menu opens. Directly under the 'Home' link is a menu item called '**Updates**'. Again, you'll see a number next to it if there are any updates available.

Click on '**Updates**' to be taken to the updates screen. This can have up to three sections. At the very top, if a WordPress update is available, you'll see an option to install it. Under

40

that, if plugins are available for update, you'll see them here. Simply check the plugins you want to update, and then click the '**Update Plugin**' button.

At the bottom of the page, if a theme has an update, you should see it listed here too (though that will depend on the theme and where you got it from). Again, check the theme(s) you want to update, and click the '**Update Themes**' button.

If you prefer to have the updates done for you automatically, check back in the plugins section of this book, where I mention a plugin called Automatic Updater that can do this for you.

9. Duplication on Category, Tag & Other Archive Pages

As mentioned at the beginning of this book, these pages are the root of many SEO problems. Let me show you an example of this.

I've created a dummy post for a fictitious gift website. The post is called 'Gift ideas for children', and it's in a category called 'children'.

After posting the article, here is my homepage:

Home   **Sample Page**

Gift ideas for children

Posted on **July 3, 2013**

These are gift ideas for children. These are gift ideas for children. These are gift ideas for children. These are gift ideas for children. These are gift ideas for children. These are gift ideas for children. These are gift ideas for children. These are gift ideas for children. These are gift ideas for children.

These are gift ideas for children. These are gift ideas for children. These are gift ideas for children. These are gift ideas for children. These are gift ideas for children. These are gift ideas for children.

These are gift ideas for children. These are gift ideas for children. These are gift ideas for children. These are gift ideas for children. These are gift ideas for children. These are gift ideas for children. These are gift ideas for children. These are gift ideas for children. These are gift ideas for children. These are gift ideas for children. These are gift ideas for children.

These are gift ideas for children. These are gift ideas for children. These are gift ideas for children. These are gift ideas for children. These are gift ideas for children.

Posted in **Children | Leave a reply**   Edit

The title of the post is actually a hyperlink that will open a page which contains an exact copy of the article. That means we now have two identical copies of the same post, but that's only the tip of the iceberg.

Look at the screenshot above under the title where it says 'Posted on July 3, 2013'. That date is a hyperlink to the date archive. Clicking on it takes me to a page that shows all posts that were published on that date. Here it is:

Home   Sample Page

Posted on July 3, 2013

Edit

Gift ideas for children

These are gift ideas for children. These are gift ideas for children. These are gift ideas for children. These are gift ideas for children. These are gift ideas for children. These are gift ideas for children. These are gift ideas for children. These are gift ideas for children. These are gift ideas for children.

These are gift ideas for children. These are gift ideas for children. These are gift ideas for children. These are gift ideas for children. These are gift ideas for children. These are gift ideas for children.

These are gift ideas for children. These are gift ideas for children. These are gift ideas for children. These are gift ideas for children. These are gift ideas for children. These are gift ideas for children. These are gift ideas for children. These are gift ideas for children. These are gift ideas for children. These are gift ideas for children. These are gift ideas for children. These are gift ideas for children.

The same full post again.

Go back to the homepage screenshot. See at the bottom of the post where it says 'Posted in children'. '**Children**' is the category, and the word 'children' is a hyperlink. If I click that, it takes me to the children category page:

43

Gift ideas for children

Posted on July 3, 2013

These are gift ideas for children. These are gift ideas for children. These are gift ideas for children. These are gift ideas for children. These are gift ideas for children. These are gift ideas for children. These are gift ideas for children. These are gift ideas for children. These are gift ideas for children.

These are gift ideas for children. These are gift ideas for children. These are gift ideas for children. These are gift ideas for children. These are gift ideas for children. These are gift ideas for children.

These are gift ideas for children. These are gift ideas for children. These are gift ideas for children. These are gift ideas for children. These are gift ideas for children. These are gift ideas for children. These are gift ideas for children. These are gift ideas for children. These are gift ideas for children. These are gift ideas for children. These are gift ideas for children.

These are gift ideas for children. These are gift ideas for children. These are gift ideas for

That page also contains the full post.

The duplication doesn't stop there. WordPress has also created an author page. If I go to the author page:

Gift ideas for children

Posted on July 3, 2013

These are gift ideas for children. These are gift ideas for children. These are gift ideas for children. These are gift ideas for children. These are gift ideas for children. These are gift ideas for children. These are gift ideas for children. These are gift ideas for children. These are gift ideas for children.

These are gift ideas for children. These are gift ideas for children. These are gift ideas for children. These are gift ideas for children. These are gift ideas for children. These are gift ideas for children.

These are gift ideas for children. These are gift ideas for children. These are gift ideas for children. These are gift ideas for children. These are gift ideas for children. These are gift ideas for children. These are gift ideas for children. These are gift ideas for children. These

Once again, we have yet another duplicated copy of the same article.

But wait, there's more! What if I added a few tags to the post? Here I've added four tags to this demo article:

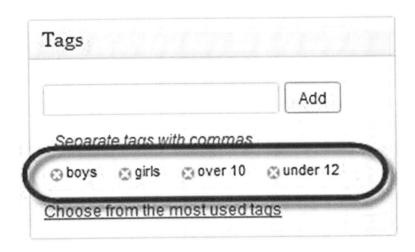

The tags are boys, girls, over 10 & under 12. These are supposed to help classify the gift ideas. However, WordPress creates a page for each of these tags, and guess what?

I'll give you a clue by showing you one of the four tag pages:

Gift ideas for children

Posted on July 3, 2013

These are gift ideas for children. These are gift ideas for children. These are gift ideas for children. These are gift ideas for children. These are gift ideas for children. These are gift ideas for children. These are gift ideas for children. These are gift ideas for children.

These are gift ideas for children. These are gift ideas for children. These are gift ideas for children. These are gift ideas for children. These are gift ideas for children. These are gift ideas for children.

Yes, that's right. The full article is published on each of the four tag pages too.

So how many times does this one post appear on the site? Well assuming I haven't missed one or two copies (something which is quite possible), we have the following:

Homepage, post page, category page, date archive, author page, and four tag pages. That's nine copies of the exact same article. And that happens with every article you publish on your site.

Now do you see why WordPress desperately needs to be SEO'd? This type of duplication can kill your rankings in Google.

If you are starting to have palpitations, thinking you have made the wrong decision choosing WordPress, relax. I'll walk you through it step by step. It really isn't so difficult to solve these problems once you know how.

10. Menus & Site Navigation

Visitors like a site with good navigation and Google likes a site that keeps its visitors happy. Of course, there is more to it than that. Good navigation on a site will help the search engines find, and even categorize your content.

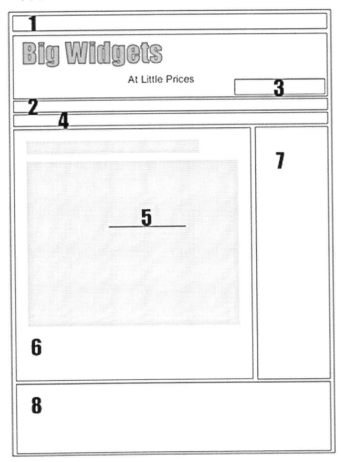

On a website, there are various places where navigation can appear. These typically include:

1. A menu above the site logo.
2. A menu below the site logo.
3. A search box in the same area as the site logo, often off to the right.
4. Breadcrumb navigation underneath the page header, but above the webpage opening header.
5. Links to other pages within the body of the content, as in-context links.
6. After the content of the page, maybe as a 'related articles' or 'You may also be interested in these' types of link lists.
7. A menu in the left and/or right sidebar.
8. A menu in the page footer.

Where you put your navigation may be determined by your choice of WordPress template. For example, some templates offer positions 1 or 2, but not both. Others offer both positions. And some may offer two navigation menus in position 2, but none in position 1.

As for the search box, this can appear in the logo area, or in the sidebar. I've even seen them in page footers. Therefore this diagram is only a rough guide.

Before we look at how to create the various forms of navigation in WordPress, let me mention one thing. Create your navigation for human visitors, not search engines. That means using the most logical and aesthetically pleasing links in the menu. Do not, under any circumstances, stuff keywords into your navigation menus and links.

For example, if you had a website about prom dresses, and had sections on your site to various brands of prom dress, you might be tempted to use something like:

- PacificPlex Prom Dresses
- Ever-Pretty Prom Dresses
- Moonar Prom Dresses
- Hot from Hollywood Prom Dresses
- US Fairytailes Prom Dresses

Notice the repetition of the words 'Prom Dresses'. Why do you think some webmasters do this? Is it to help their visitors? Well, considering the whole site is about prom dresses, I'd assume not. This is done purely for the search engines for two reasons:

1. In this menu, the phrase 'prom dresses' appears five times in the hope that the page would rank better for that term. In the good old days of pre-2011 SEO, this would have worked. Today it's more likely to get you a Penguin penalty.
2. Each item in the menu will link to a page on the site. That link uses anchor text (the text you as the visitor see for any given link). In this type of menu, the keyword-stuffed anchor text is there as an attempt to boost the rankings of the page the link points to for its anchor text phrase. Say if this site had 100 pages, each using the same prom dress menu. This means each of the five pages in the menu would have 100 links pointing to them. That's 100 of the exact same anchor texts. Again, pre-2011, this worked. Today it does not, and this tactic will come back to bite you (or do Penguins nip?).

TIP: Look at the 'SEO' on your site. If you cannot say with 100% that you have done it in your visitor's best interests, then get rid of it. This goes for site navigation, content, and internal linking between pages, etc.

OK, with that said, how do you implement navigation into WordPress?

Well, there are a number of different ways.

You can use plugins. You can also use the menu system built into WordPress.

In many cases you will know exactly which links you want in a navigation area. These links are usually fixed and rarely change. In this instance, I recommend you use the menu system built into WordPress.

On other occasions, you might want a list of the most recent posts, or posts related specifically to the current one. These menus are constantly changing as new content gets added to the site, and are therefore best handled with plugins.

10.1. Recommended Navigation

Let me make the recommendations first, and then I'll show you how to implement them.

To start off (you can add or change this later), I suggest that you have the following four navigation features:

1. **One menu:** Either above or below the site logo, or in the footer, where there are links to your 'legal pages'. That's the Contact, Privacy, Disclaimers, About Us, and so forth. These links should be 'nofollowed', and the actual legal pages should be set to 'noindex', 'Follow' and 'No Archive'.
2. **A search box:** If your theme supports a search box in the header area, you might want it there. However, I personally prefer a search box at the top of the sidebar (right or left, whichever I use).
3. **A main navigation menu:** Either in or below the logo or in the sidebar (right or left), that links to the main sections of your website (the main categories).
4. **Sidebar dynamic menus:** Each category (or main section), of your site should have a different navigation menu in the sidebar. Google likes dynamic menus which change depending where on a site a visitor is. For example, if you are in the mountain bike section of a site, the main navigation menu should be related to mountain bikes. If you are in the road bike section, the main navigation menu relates to road bikes.

Personally, the type of sites I build also benefit from a 'related posts' section, either after the main content of a post, or in the sidebar (done using the 'Yet Another Related Posts' plugin). However, it depends on the type of site you build, so this may not suite your particular project. I also implement internal linking between the posts on the site using context-sensitive links (this is done using the 'C.I. Backlinks' plugin). The internal linking of posts on a site is something that most of the big players do (see Wikipedia for example), and it really does help your pages get indexed and rank better.

10.2. Implementing the Four Main Navigation Features

Let's look at the 'legal menu' first.

10.2.1. Implementing Legal Menus

If you login to the Dashboard and go to Appearance -> Menus, you'll be able to create a menu that contains links to your legal pages.

I won't go through the details of creating individual menus here, as that is covered in my WordPress for Beginners book (http://www.amazon.com/dp/B009ZVO3H6). However, I will show you how to make the links in the navigation menu 'nofollow'.

Pull down the Screen Options (top right of the Dashboard), and make sure that '**Link Relationship (XFN)**' is checked.

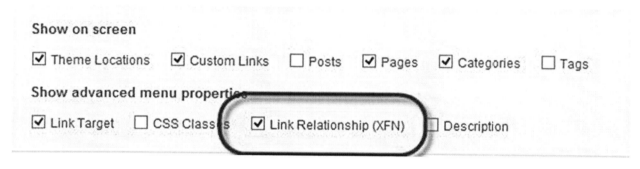

You can now expand the items in your menu:

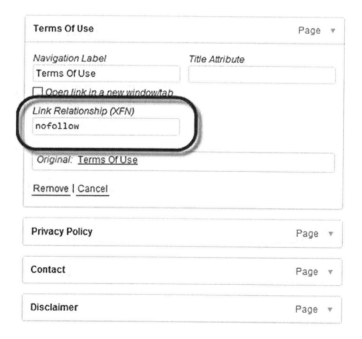

Type the word **nofollow** into the link relationship box.

Repeat this for all your legal pages; and don't forget to save your menu.

Once you have the menu saved, you can then insert it into the header area, or the sidebar. To do this, look to top left of the 'Menus' screen and you'll see a section called **'Theme Locations'**.

These are defined by your theme, and you'll see one or two locations available. For most themes, these theme locations are above and below the logo, which is exactly what we want.

The theme I am using in the screenshot above is the Genesis Lifestyle theme. Primary Navigation Menu is above the Logo, and the Secondary Navigation Menu is below it.

To place the legal menu in the header area of the page, simply select the menu you created from the dropdown box, in the position you want it to appear i.e., Primary or Secondary Navigation.

OK, so how do you add the menu to the footer?

Well, with Genesis themes, this is easy.

Go to the Appearance -> Widgets screen. You should see a **'Custom Menu'** widget available. You'll also see a footer area (or three), on the right hand side. Simply drag the Custom Menu Widget into the Footer Widget area, and then select the legal menu:

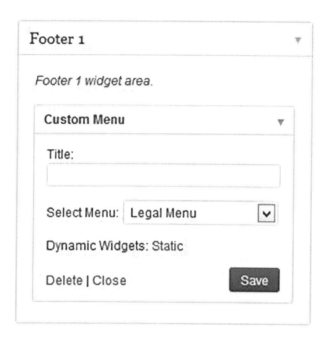

This will then display the legal menu in your site's footer:

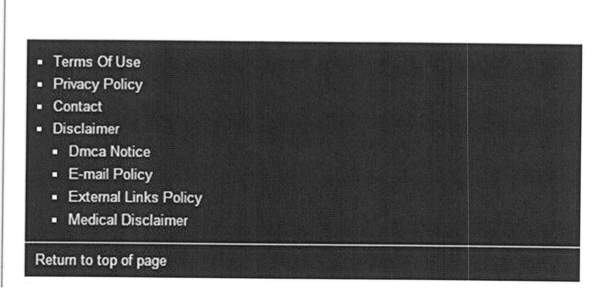

Again, all links will be nofollow because we set that up in the actual menu.

However, there is one other task we need to do. That is to make sure our legal pages are setup so that they are 'noindex', 'Follow', and 'No Archive'. Fortunately, this is easy with the WordPress SEO plugin we installed earlier.

Go to each of your legal pages in turn and open them in the editor (Pages -> All Pages, then click on the title of the page in the list).

The WordPress SEO plugin has added a section to all post/page edit screens. It's labelled as **WordPress SEO by Yoast** and it has three tabs. We want to select the '**Advanced**' tab:

Select '**noindex**' from the dropdown box at the top, '**Follow**' from the radio button, and '**No Archive**' from the list box.

Now click the '**Update**' button to save the changes.

Repeat this procedure for all other legal pages (and pages/posts that you don't want to appear in the search engines).

OK, now you have a legal menu on your site, with links set as nofollow, and the pages themselves set as noindex. These two settings will prevent Google from indexing pages that are not important to your site, and thus stop valuable Page Rank from flowing to these pages, meaning more link juice for your important content.

10.2.2. Implementing a Search Box

WordPress comes with a search widget, so you can start off by using that. They aren't actually very good, so I recommend you eventually switch to using a Google custom search (search Google for instructions when you are ready), but the WordPress search feature will do to get you started.

Simply drag the 'Search' widget to the widgetized area where you want it to appear. In some themes you'll get a 'Header Right' option. This is to insert a widget into the right hand side of the logo area. You can drag the search box widget there if you want to. Alternatively, drag it to the top of the main or primary sidebar.

You can enter a title for the widget if you like. The title will then appear right above the search box. However, since most people are used to seeing a box with a search button, the title isn't strictly necessary, it's personal preference.

10.2.3. Main Site Navigation Menu

The main site navigation is inserted into the sidebar in exactly the same way we saw the legal menu inserted into the site. Drag and drop a 'Custom Menu' widget into the area you want your main navigation to appear. I nearly always put it in the main sidebar. Now, the last type of navigation I suggested you use is dynamic navigation. That means the navigation that points to the main sections (categories), on your site, and will probably only appear on the homepage. Once you are in other areas of the site, you'll use a different navigation menu. Let's look and see how we do that.

10.2.4. Dynamic Navigation Menus

To achieve dynamic menus, we need the 'Dynamic Widgets' plugin that we installed earlier. When this is installed, EVERY widget you add in the Appearance -> Widgets section of the dashboard has a new feature:

See the **Dynamic Widgets: Static**?

That word 'Static' is a hyperlink that takes you to the settings for the widget. From there you get to specify exactly where on the site you want the widget to appear.

The default setting is 'Static', which means the widget appears on every page & post of the entire site, but you can change the default. Say you only want the widget to appear on the homepage, then the word 'Static' changes to 'Dynamic', and you'll get a few other details in the widget area showing you what 'Dynamic' settings you are using.

Assuming you have already created a main navigation menu that links to the main categories of the site, let's set it to only appear on the homepage.

Open the '**Custom Menu**' in the widget area:

Click the '**Static**' link.

This opens up a large page of options.

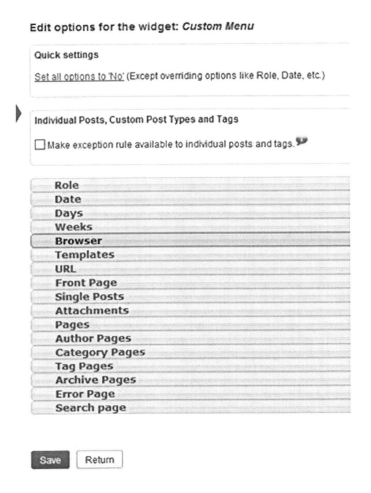

Each of these 'horizontal bars' will open up if you click on them.

Since we only want the menu to appear on the homepage, the first thing we need to do is click the link at the top of these options: **Set all options to 'No'**.

If we now click on any one of these bars, it will expand, showing us that it is set to 'No'.

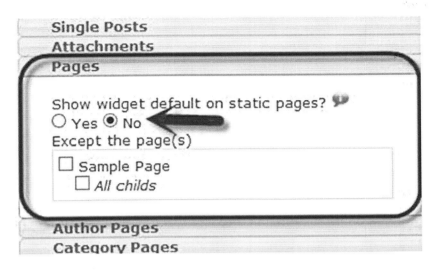

This means the widget will not appear anywhere on the site. We need to fix this by opening up the homepage options (called 'Front Page' in this plugin), and select '**Yes**'.

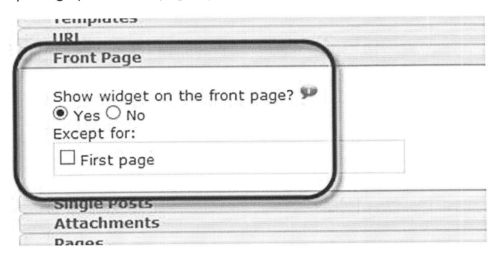

Now, don't forget to save the settings by clicking the '**Save**' button at the bottom. This will then return you to the widgets area of the Dashboard.

If you look at the Custom Menu widget, you'll see that additional information I told you about:

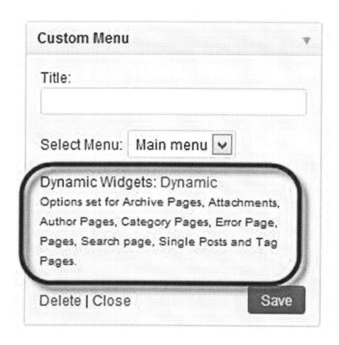

The word 'Static' now reads 'Dynamic', and we can see that the options have been set for various pages on the site.

If you check your site, you will find the main navigation menu only appears on the homepage.

To get dynamic menus for each specific area of our site, we need to setup the menu in the Appearance -> Menu section. For example, if you have five categories on your site, set up five Custom Menus, and include the most relevant menu items for each category.

Next, add all of these custom menus to the sidebar, and then go into them, one by one, and change the settings for where they should appear on your site.

For this example, let's assume I want the custom menu to appear only in the '**Hot from Hollywood**' category (that's the category page plus any posts in that category).

Step one will be to click the link to set all options to 'No', just as we did for the homepage. Next we need to change two settings.

The first is in the '**Category Pages**' settings:

Category Pages ✓

Show widget default on category pages?
○ Yes ● No
Except the categories

☐ Ever-Pretty
  ☐ *All childs*
☑ Hot from Hollywood
  ☐ *All childs*
☐ Moonar
  ☐ *All childs*
☐ Pacificflex
  ☐ *All childs*
☐ US Fairytailes
  ☐ *All childs*

Select '**No**' at the top, and then check the '**Hot from Hollywood**' checkbox. This may sound counter-intuitive, but read the information on the plugin settings screen. We are checking the Hot from Hollywood category so that it will be the exception. We don't want the widget to appear on category pages EXCEPT the one(s) that are checked.

OK, once saved, that will show the menu on the 'Hot from Hollywood' category page. We also need to make it appear on the posts within that category, so we have to set the '**Single Posts**' options.

Single Posts ✓

Show widget default on single posts? 💬
○ Yes ◉ No

Except the author(s)

☐ Maria

Except the categories

☐ Ever-Pretty
  ☐ *All childs*
☑ Hot from Hollywood
  ☑ *All childs*
☐ Moonal
  ☐ *All childs*
☐ Pacificflex
  ☐ *All childs*
☐ US Fairytailes
  ☐ *All childs*

Again, we select '**No**' at the top because we don't want this widget appearing on posts, except the ones we check

The 'Hot from Hollywood' category is selected, but you also have the option to check *'All childs'*, which will mean any 'Hot from Hollywood' sub-categories will also have this menu.

OK, once done, save your changes.

The menu will only appear on the 'Hot from Hollywood' category page AND all the posts within that category.

You can explore the other settings for the dynamic widgets plugin. You will see an enormous level of control over which pages your widgets appear on.

Using the techniques shown in this chapter, you can easily create custom sidebars, and custom footers, etc, with any type of widget in any area that is widgetized.

This is the easiest way to create dynamic navigation systems on your website. Don't forget, besides navigation systems, you can also serve up custom adverts, custom subscription boxes, custom videos, etc., and all on different sections of the site.

11. A Custom Logo for Your Header?

By default, WordPress displays your site name and tagline (configured in the Settings -> General Settings menu), as the logo for the site.

While the default site name and tagline may be OK for most projects, they often don't give the best impression to your visitors. And since a lot of modern SEO is all about keeping the visitor happy, you may want to create (or have created for you), a professional image logo and use that instead. Remember, you never get a second chance to make that first impression!

While it's beyond the scope of this book to show you how to create a logo, I can show you how to use a custom logo image on your site, but how you achieve this will vary somewhat between themes.

Go to the Appearance -> Themes menu:

You will see your selected theme active at the top (I'm using the default Twenty Twelve theme for this demonstration). There is more than likely a 'Header' link here. This will take you to your site's header options, so click on it.

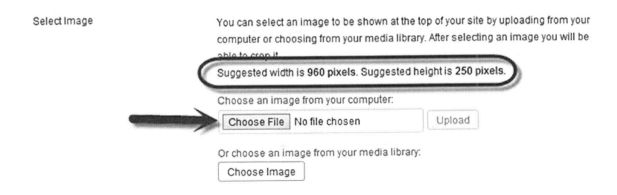

61

You should be given a suggested logo dimension. The dimensions for the Twenty Twelve theme are 960 pixels by 250 pixels. Make sure you create your logo using the *exact dimensions* as recommended by your theme, or you may have to crop it once it's uploaded.

You can select the logo from your computer or from your WordPress Media Library, if you uploaded it there. If you select an image logo from your computer, make sure you click the '**Upload**' button after selecting the file.

The only other thing you need to do is remove the default logo text. There is a check box that you simply need to uncheck:

Make sure you save changes when done. Your new logo should now be active site-wide.

12. Comment System

The comment systems and how to integrate them into your site, is an important, yet often over-looked piece of the on-site SEO puzzle.

The comments on your site are VERY important. A lot of comments tell visitors that your site is busy. If it's busy, then it's likely to be trusted by more people. If it's trusted, it will do better in Google too.

However, all of this is dependent on having good quality comments. Comments need to add to the 'conversation' that has gone before them. Put more specifically, do the comments add to the original article, either by way of an opinion, additional information, or a question? Another good type of comment is when a visitor replies to someone else's remarks, but again, only if those replies are adding to the conversation. These are the types of comments you need to try and get on your site.

When a website is new, it's all too easy to approve poor comments just to make the site look visited. Don't do it! Never approve a comment *unless* it actually adds something to the post topic and conversation already on-going, that's if there are other comments of course.

Typical comments you should NOT approve include the congratulatory comments, like "Well done!", or "Great post". Even "Thanks for writing about this topic in a way I can understand". Although the latter might sound sincere, it adds absolutely nothing to the conversation because there is no reference to the topic in question.

Get used to approving only the best comments. Even if you don't get very many to begin with (which is quite possible), great comments add value to the overall visitor experience of your website. Or to put it another way, a website full of poor & spammy comments will put your visitors off and they won't have much confidence in you or the credibility of your site.

13. RSS Feeds

WordPress automatically creates several RSS feeds for your site.

You can access the main feed for your site by adding **/feed** to the end of your domain URL.

The feed for my SEO website is: **ezSEONews.com/feed**.

We setup the RSS feed earlier to show just 10 posts, and only the title and excerpts of those. Therefore, the main feed will show the last 10 posts you published on your site.

WordPress also creates six other feeds:

1. Comments – this feed shows the last 10 comments made on your site.
2. Post-specific feeds – which show the last 10 comments made on a particular post.
3. Category feeds – which show the last 10 posts made in a particular category.
4. Tag feeds – which show the last 10 posts using a particular tag.
5. Author feeds – showing the last 10 posts made by a particular author.
6. Search feeds – showing the search results for a particular keyword phrase.

I won't go into details showing you how to find all of these feeds. If you are interested, you can read the WordPress codex article on this topic:

http://codex.wordpress.org/WordPress_Feeds

From an SEO point of view, feeds are interesting. For example, there are a number of RSS feed submission services where you can get backlinks to your site by submitting your feed(s). Whenever you add fresh content, these feeds get updated, linking back to the new page. In terms of helping pages rank higher, these types of links won't do much good, but they can get your new content indexed a lot quicker. What I would suggest here is not to overdo this type of submission. Pick maybe three or four of the top RSS feed sites, and submit a feed to each (you can choose different feeds for each if you want).

One thing I like to use feeds for is adding a recent posts section to my site's sidebar, or footer. WordPress comes with a feed widget, and all you need to do is supply the feed URL for it to work.

For example, on my SEO site, I have a category on Kindle Publishing. I can grab the feed URL for that category:

http://ezseonews.com/seo/kindle-publishing/feed/

I then add it to an RSS widget by using the Dynamic Widget plugin we saw earlier. This will only show that RSS feed on other posts in the Kindle Publishing category.

Here is the widget set up:

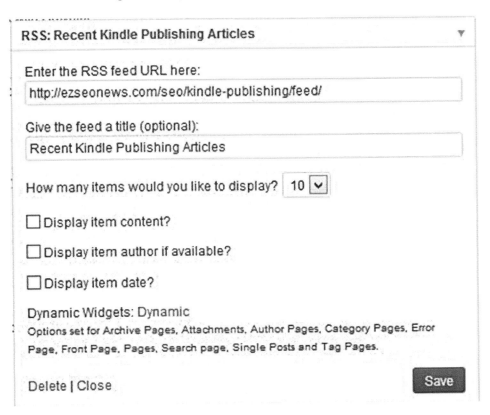

Here is the widget in action on the 'Kindle Publishing' articles (and category), pages.

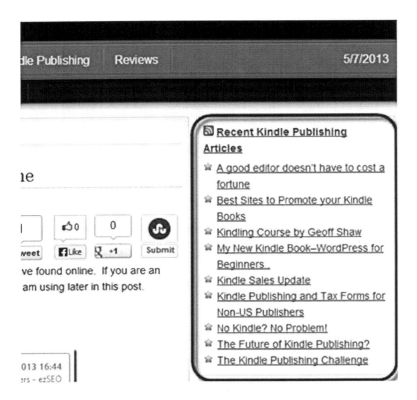

This has a couple of benefits:

1. You can highlight other recent articles in a given category. If someone is reading an article about one aspect of Kindle publishing, the chances are these other articles will be of interest too.
2. From an SEO perspective, this is good because you have inter-linking of the Kindle publishing articles, each reinforcing the theme of your pages and providing spiderable links to the other articles in the 'silo'.

14. Google Authorship & WordPress User Profiles

Google is always updating its algorithm. There are hundreds of minor updates every year, with some major ones sprinkled in between. In the last couple of years, we've had to contend with Panda, Penguin and then Penguin 2.0 (which was a major upgrade to the original). All of these updates have been necessary, because Google has faced a constant battle with webmasters trying to game the system; that is webmasters who want their content to rank #1 in the Google search results pages.

We all want to be ranked #1 for various search phrases - obviously - but we don't all deserve these top slot(s). Google has a problem with webmasters that try to force their content to the top of the first page. Google wants total control. They need to be able to decide which content deserves to be at the top, and not leave that up to webmasters, who can, and do, try all manner of techniques to get these valuable positions.

One of the most abused SEO techniques over the years has been link building. The general principle has always been more is better. Webmasters have always considered link building to be a safe practice because you cannot control who links to your site. Google themselves even told us once that links could not hurt a site's rankings.

I guess the search giant finally snapped, because today, bad links can cause you ranking problems. To help webmasters fix link problems, Google introduced the disavow tool. You can use this to list those links pointing at your site which you do not approve of. This now means that site owners have full control over the links to their pages, signifying Google have shifted the responsibility of bad links away from their algorithm, and onto the webmaster. In other words, if you have bad links pointing at your site, it is *your* fault as far as Google is concerned.

While the Google vs. Webmasters battle has raged on all these years, Google has been constantly looking for other 'signals' they could use to help them better rank web pages. The holy grail of 'signals' would be one that webmasters could not manipulate to their advantage, and they may have just come up with the answer.

14.1. Google Authorship

Google introduced 'Google Authorship' as a way to connect a piece of content with its true author. By setting up Google authorship, and using it properly, you can tell Google about all of the content you have scattered around the internet.

So you might be asking how this could be used as a ranking factor. Well, let's consider a couple of scenarios.

Peter is an expert in alternative medicine. He has his own website, but also contributes to several industry leading websites with regular articles. His writings are excellent, they get good traffic, and there is a lot of social interaction with visitors. With Google authorship, Peter can tell Google about all of his content, and Google can do the rest. They will be monitoring the 'feedback' from visitors to Peter's pages around the web, and be able to assign him an 'author rank'. Now, what if Google decided that any new article written by Peter deserved to rank higher, simply because he had become a trusted author?

OK, let's now take the example of Sean. He's a marketer and has his hands in lots of pies. He has multiple websites based in health 'niches', and submits content around the web to various other websites and blogs which accept guest posts. But because Sean is not an expert, his articles don't appear on the top industry websites, so he had to settle with making his presence known on lower quality ones.

Google knows all about Sean's websites, which have low traffic and high bounce rates. In addition, the guest posts Sean has been making are on sites that have a lot of ads. In fact, those sites are setup specifically to make money with AdSense, and the owner accepts just about any article from anyone, which is why they accept Sean's pieces. Because of this, visitors also don't spend long reading his articles on any of these sites either. Sean's 'author rank' is not great, so when Google notices another one of his articles, they don't give him a boost in rankings, in fact they push his new content even further down the SERPs.

Is Author Rank Real?

Right now? Probably not. In the near future? Probably so. We need to remember that Google authorship is still a relatively new concept, and there are a lot of problems Google needs to sort out before they'd trust author rank as a major part of their algorithm.

What we do know is that in 2011, shortly after Google Authorship was released, Google engineer, Othar Hansson, mentioned that they may use data collected from Google authorship to help rank content. In addition to this, at the Edinburgh International TV Festival, Eric Schmidt (who, at the time was CEO of Google), suggested that Google+ could be used as an 'identity rank' (http://bit.ly/vPmvAp), which ultimately could sort out the good authors from the bad.

Whether it exists now or not, I believe it will be an important ranking factor at some point in the future, so I encourage you to establish your authorship for the content that you create.

There are several other advantages for implementing Google Authorship, even if author rank isn't one of them – yet!

- See your photo next to your entries in the SERPs. This not only builds your brand, but it also catches the eye of the web searcher, so...
- An image in the SERPs, next to a listing, can increase click through rates.
- People searching Google will be able to add you to their Google circles, or find out more about you by visiting your Google profile, all from within the search result listing.

Often there will be a 'more...' link next to the entry in the SERPs, which opens up a custom search showing more of that author's content.

14.2. Setting up Google Authorship

There are a couple of ways to do this, depending on whether you have control of the site your content is appearing on or not. You can read instructions from Google to learn more:

https://plus.google.com/authorship

14.2.1. The Process, Step-by-step If You Own the Domain

Step 1: You first need to have a Google plus account. If you have a Gmail address, then you just need to claim your Google plus profile. To do this, go to:

https://plus.google.com/

Login with your Gmail login details and follow the instructions to get set up with Google Plus.

IMPORTANT: Please note that you should only have ONE Google plus account, so use your main Gmail address. Although discussing the use of Google plus is beyond the scope of this book, I can tell you that you can setup Google Pages for each site you own. What this means is that you can effectively manage multiple sites from within a single Google profile.

Step 2: Upload a profile picture, making sure your face is clear. If you don't have a clear headshot, Google will not show your image in the SERPs.

If you want a short primer on Google+, read this post here:

(http://www.orbitmedia.com/blog/google-plus-guide).

Step 3: Login to Google+, and go to your profile page (click your image top right and select '**View Profile**'). Now go to the '**About**' page. There is a section labelled '**Contact Information**' on the 'About' page. Click the edit link and add your email address.

Step 4: While this step should be unnecessary, I recommend you do it nonetheless.

On the '**About**' page of your profile ('About' link located top left), there is a section labelled '**Links**'. Click the edit button and add your website's homepage URL to the '**Contributor to**' section.

Before you leave your Google Plus profile, grab the URL in the browser address bar.

Step 5: Now login to your WordPress Dashboard, and go to Users -> Your Profile.

Scroll down and you'll see a box for your Google + profile URL:

Yahoo IM	
Jabber / Google Talk	
Google+	232271221234192246/about?hl=en&partnerid=gplp0
Twitter username (without @)	
Facebook profile URL	

You will notice that the Google plus URL has some parameters at the end.

You can delete everything after the final '/', so in my screenshot, I'd delete from **about?hl=......** to the end of that line.

You also need to make sure that the field '**Display name publicly as**' is set to the exact same name as your Google+ profile:

Name

Username	Andy
First Name	Andy
Last Name	Williams
Nickname *(required)*	Andy
Display name publicly as	Andy Williams ▾

Now go to the SEO menu, and click on '**Social**'.

This takes you to the WordPress SEO settings for social features. Click on the Google+ tab, and select your author name from the top drop down box:

You do not need to enter your Google + profile URL here. By selecting your name, the plugin adds a rel=author tag to your homepage, so Google plus knows it's yours.

The pages on your website now link to your Google + profile, and your profile links to your site. Authorship should now be established, so let's go and check it using the Google Rich Snippet testing tool:

http://www.google.com/webmasters/tools/richsnippets

Enter your homepage URL, and click the preview button:

Structured Data Testing Tool

| URL | HTML |

http://ezseonews.com/review/kindling-course-by-geoff-shaw/   PREVIEW

Select the HTML tab to view the retrieved HTML and experiment with adjusting it.

Google search results   Google Custom Search

Preview

Kindling Course by Geoff Shaw - ezSEO Newsletter
ezseonews.com/review/kindling-course-by-geoff-shaw/
by Andy Williams - More by Andy Williams
The excerpt from the page will show up here. The reason we can't show text from your webpage is because the text depends on the query the user types.

Your Google plus profile image should now show up next to your entry preview.

14.2.2. What About Guest Posts?

If you are likely to have content on websites you don't actually own, how can you tell Google you wrote those articles?

Well, this is quite easy, providing the site that hosts your content allows you to enter HTML into your articles.

Step 1: Add the guest post site to your Google Plus '**contributor to**' section (See step 4 of the previous section if you need a recap).

If it's a one-off post on the site, you can link directly to the post itself. If you have (or intend to have), several posts on a particular site, you can link to its homepage URL.

Step 2: Link your guest post to your Google profile using the following code:

<a href="**GOOGLEPLUSURL**?rel=author">Google+</a>

Just swap the **GOOGLEPLUSURL** part with your actual profile URL.

Now go and check your guest post in the Rich Snippet Testing tool.

14.3. Gravatars & the Author Bio on Your Site

Since you've bothered to add your profile image next to your pages in the SERPs, doesn't it also make sense to add that profile image to the pages on your site? This also helps build brand, but not only that. People like to know who they are dealing with, and a face behind the name adds trust and credibility to your site(s) too.

The first step in adding a photo to your posts is to sign up for a Gravatar:

(https://en.gravatar.com/).

When you get there, you'll see a box where you can add your email address. You need to enter the *exact* same one that you used for your WordPress site.

You will then be asked to '**Sign in with WordPress.com**'. If you don't have an account with WordPress.com, then you can sign up for one there first.

OK, now all you have to do is just follow the on-screen instructions.

Once your account has been setup, you can upload an image and connect your email address to that photo. Be sure to use the same image that you have in your Google Plus profile. It's better for branding to use the same image on our site as the one that shows up in the SERPs.

You can add multiple email addresses to your Gravatar account, so if you control lots of sites, or have many email addresses, you can assign the same (or different), image to every email you'd like a Gravatar for.

Once this is setup, if you leave comments on blogs that have Gravatars enabled (btw, most of them do), then your image will show up next to your comments (assuming you entered the same email address when submitting them). Some forums also use Gravatars for images, so as you can see, we have multiple ways to brand ourselves and build trust around the web.

14.3.1. Genesis Users

To setup the author bio on your posts, login to the dashboard and go to the Users -> Your profile page.

About Yourself

Biographical Info

> Dr. Andy Williams is a Science teacher by training, but has now been working online for over a decade, specializing in search engine optimization and affiliate marketing. He publishes his free weekly <a href="http://ezseonews.com/">Internet Marketing newsletter</a> with tips, advice, tutorials, and more.
> You can subscribe to his free daily paper called the <a

Share a little biographical information to fill out your profile. This may be shown publicly.

In the '**Biographical info**' box, enter the bio that you want to appear for each post on your site.

Now scroll down a little to the '**Author box**' section.

This text will be the first paragraph, and display o

Author Box

☑ Enable Author Box on this User's Posts?
☑ Enable Author Box on this User's Archives?

Enable both check boxes.

This adds the author box to individual posts, and also the author archive page.

Here is the author box after one of my posts:

5. EzSEO Newsletter #342

   TweetIn this issue: 1. My New Kindle Book is Free for 5 days 2. Is Google going to penalize ALL
   WordPress sites? 3. My Kindle Sales Update. 4. Kindle Publishing & Tax Forms for Non-US Publishers
   5. XHeader Demo – Creating a Header Graphic for your Site. 6. Domain Registrars & Hosting
   Companies Hi Again [...]

FILED UNDER: EZSEO NEWSLETTERS

About Andy Williams
Dr. Andy Williams is a Science teacher by training, but has now been working online for
over a decade, specializing in search engine optimization and affiliate marketing. He
publishes his free weekly Internet Marketing newsletter with tips, advice, tutorials, and
more.
You can subscribe to his free daily paper called the Google Daily and follow him
on Facebook orTwitter. You can also follow me on Google +

Comments

Moto Akumulator says:
4/7/2013 at 14:20 (Edit)

Youre now book is reference reading for me, as always. Thanks for gift I Will sure post a

14.3.2. Non-Genesis Users

For non-Genesis users, you'll need to see whether or not your template has an author
bio box feature. If it does, you can use that. If it doesn't, there are some plugins that
add this functionality to any WordPress site. I cannot recommend any particular
plugin as I don't use one. You should be able to find some by searching the WordPress
plugin directory (http://wordpress.org/plugins/).

15. Robots.txt File

The robots.txt file is a plain text file that contains various instructions for the search engines. It includes details on specific folders and files that the search engines should, or should not spider.

For example, you can tell the search engines to ignore all files within a specific folder on your server. A good example of a folder that search engines should keep out of is the WordPress plugin folder. The files there are not content pages on your site, so why would you want the search engines sniffing around in there? If you allow them to, they'll index the PHP files in those folders, and so list them in the SERPS as content on your site. Not really what we want is it?

Using a robots.txt file is easy enough. Just create a text file in any text editor, and add in the commands. Once done, simply upload it to the root folder of your WordPress site.

On the WordPress website, they show a suggested example robots.txt file. You can find it here:

http://codex.wordpress.org/Search_Engine_Optimization_for_WordPress

However, since we are using Yoast's WordPress plugin, a lot of what we need to do in terms of excluding search engine spiders, is done for us. In a post on the subject (http://yoast.com/example-robots-txt-wordpress/), Joost de Valk (the author of the WordPress SEO plugin), goes through the WordPress example and explains why most of it is not really necessary.

In Yoast's article, he suggests a much simplified robots.txt file, and it's similar to the one he currently uses on Yoast.com. Here it is:

User-Agent: *
Disallow: /wp-content/plugins/

I personally add a couple of extra lines to mine. The first one is to disallow spiders from going into the cgi-bin folder:

Disallow: /cgi-bin

The majority of site owners never have any files and sub-directories in this folder anyway, so it's not critical for most. The other line I add to my robots.txt file is one that tells the spiders where my sitemap is located.

You can find the location of your sitemap by going into the XML Sitemap settings found in the SEO menu in the left sidebar.

 Yoast WordPress SEO: XML Sitemaps

XML Sitemap

☑ Check this box to enable XML sitemap functionality.

You can find your XML Sitemap here: | XML Sitemap |

You do **not** need to generate the XML sitemap, nor will it take up time to generate after

Click the '**XML Sitemap**' button and your sitemap will open in the browser:

XML Sitemap

Generated by **Yoast's WordPress SEO plugin**, this is an XML Sitemap, meant 1

You can find more information about XML sitemaps on **sitemaps.org**.

This XML Sitemap Index file contains 3 sitemaps.

Sitemap	Last Modified
http://███████████com/post-sitemap.xml	2013-07-04 07:16
http://███████████com/page-sitemap.xml	2013-07-04 07:25
http://███████████com/category-sitemap.xml	2013-07-04 07:16

You now have a choice. You can copy the URL from the address bar of your internet browser and use that as your sitemap URL. Alternatively, you can grab the URLs of the individual sitemaps listed below, and add each one separately to your robots.txt file.

I like to add all three (you could have more or less), sitemaps to my robots.txt file.

Those lines look like this:

Sitemap: http://mydomain.com/post-sitemap.xml

Obviously I've switched my real domain in that URL. My complete robots.txt file therefore looks like this:

User-Agent: *
Disallow: /wp-content/plugins/
Disallow: /cgi-bin
Allow: /wp-content/uploads

Sitemap: http://mydomain.com/post-sitemap.xml
Sitemap: http://mydomain.com/page-sitemap.xml
Sitemap: http://mydomain.com/category-sitemap.xml

After saving this as a plain text file called **robots.txt**, just upload it to your site's root folder (this is where WordPress is installed).

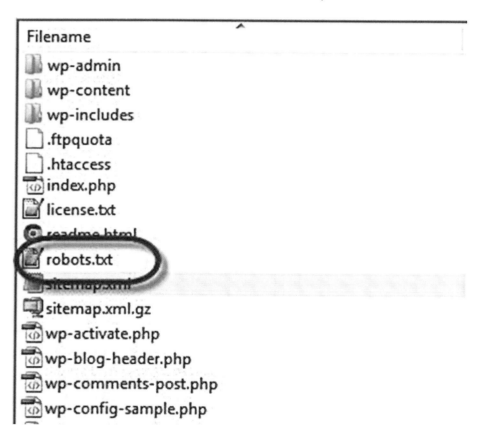

In the screenshot above, you can see the robots.txt file in the same folder as the wp-admin, wp-content & wp-includes folder. Seeing these folders simply confirms I have uploaded it to the correct place.

16. WWW or No WWW?

You see some websites with the 'www.' prefix, and others without. Google actually treats these as different URLs. When you have links pointing to your site, you need them to all show the same, either with the www. or without it.

You therefore need to decide which way you want your site's URL to be displayed.

Once WordPress is installed, visit your homepage by typing in the www. version of the domain. See what WordPress does by default. More often than not, it will be the non-www version and you will be automatically redirected there. So even if you type in the www. of the URL, it won't show once the page loads.

My advice is to use whatever WordPress shows you by default, unless you have a good reason to want the other version.

Once decided on your preferred version, login to your WordPress Dashboard and go to the Settings -> General screen

| WordPress Address (URL) | http://ezseonews.com |
| Site Address (URL) | http://ezseonews.com |

Enter the address here if you want your site homepage to b

Now you need to tell Google which version you want to use. You can do this in Google Webmaster Tools, so login to your GWT account, and click on the site you are working on.

Now click on the cog icon located in the top right, and select '**Site Settings**'.

In the screen that loads, you can select the correct version of your site by selecting the '**Preferred domain**' radio button:

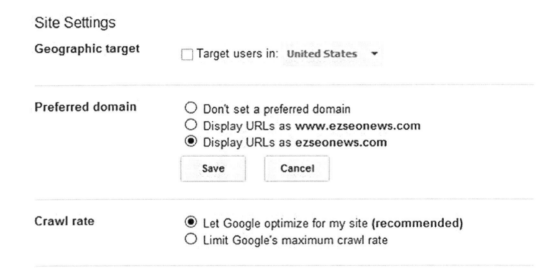

Note, that you can also select the '**Geographic target**' for your site on this screen. Just check the box and select your preferred target location.

If your site is for a worldwide audience, then leave this box unchecked. However, if your site is really only for the UK, as one example, then check the box and select the United Kingdom from the drop down. This asks Google to give your site preferential treatment on the UK Google. However, that doesn't automatically mean you'll rank better there.

17. Pages Versus Posts

While I covered this in my WordPress for Beginners book, it is important you understand the basics, so I'll go over fundamentals again here.

One of the things that many WordPress beginners get confused about is the difference between WordPress Pages and WordPress Posts. What makes things even more confusing is the tendency to call any web page a 'page', even if it is actually a 'post'.

To try to make things clearer, when I am referring to a web page loaded in your browser, whether it's been created as a WordPress post or a WordPress page, I'll call it a web page. If I am specifically talking about a WordPress post or a WordPress page, then I'll make sure I prefix the words post and page with 'WordPress'.

Here is a quick key:

Web page: Any web page that's loaded in your internet browser.

WordPress Page: Content created as a WordPress 'Page'.

WordPress Post: Content created as a WordPress 'Post'.

Got it?

OK, let's carry on.

With WordPress, we need to make the distinction between WordPress pages and WordPress posts, as they are both different and have distinctive purposes.

Let's look at the features of these two:

17.1. Posts

- Can be displayed chronologically or in reverse chronological order in a number of places on your site, including author pages, category pages, most recent posts, and RSS feeds.
- They are assigned to categories.
- They can be tagged.
- Posts can allow visitor comments.
- Posts appear in your site's RSS feeds and can therefore be syndicated to email subscribers if using a service like FeedBurner.

- Posts can have excerpts, which is basically a short summary of the written piece. These can be used by WordPress and plugins to supply a Meta Description tag, and short descriptions of posts in related posts features, etc.
- Posts do not have a custom template feature. There was a feature introduced in WordPress 3.1 called 'Post Formats'. Not all themes support these, but they are available to all theme developers if they wish to use them. Basically, this feature allows posts to be classified as: *standard, aside, audio, chat, gallery, link, quote, status* or *video*, and their appearance changes depending on the post format. You can read more about post format here: http://codex.wordpress.org/Post_Formats

17.2. Pages

- These are 'static' and not listed or sorted by date order. They are, however, hierarchical, so you can have a parent page with several child pages.
- Pages are not put into categories.
- Pages do not have tags.
- Although it is possible to enable comments on pages, this isn't typically something you want to do.
- Pages do not appear in your site's RSS feed and are therefore not syndicated to email subscribers when using FeedBurner.
- Pages do not have excerpts.
- Pages can use a 'custom template' feature making it possible to vary the appearance of them (read your template documentation to see what is available).
- You can setup a WordPress page to be used as your homepage.

17.3. When to Use WordPress Pages, and WordPress Posts

As you can see, there are several distinct differences between the two.

In terms of SEO, Google doesn't care whether a web page is created as a WordPress page or a WordPress post. However, the features we have available with WordPress posts make them the obvious choice for content that we hope to rank well for in the SERPs. Because of this, I recommend you use WordPress pages and WordPress posts as follows:

Use WordPress pages for the 'legal pages' (disclaimers, privacy statement, contact, about us, etc), and use WordPress posts for everything else.

When I say everything else, I am referring to all content that is written to engage the visitor. If it's something you want a visitor to read, and maybe comment on or share to their own social circles, definitely use a post.

By sticking to this simple rule, you can take advantage of the way WordPress was designed to work, and thus get maximum SEO benefits out of it.

The only exception I make to this rule is when I want to setup my homepage using a WordPress page, rather than one which displays the last 10 WordPress posts (more on this in the next chapter).

18. Setting up the Homepage

There are two main ways of setting up a homepage in WordPress. You can either create a WordPress page for it, or you can base your homepage to display the latest WordPress posts.

You make that decision in the **Settings -> Reading** options.

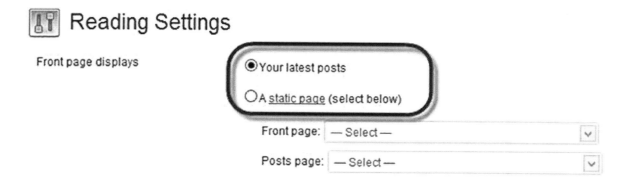

Essentially, using a WordPress pages for your homepage means you can have a more 'static' front page, i.e., one that doesn't change too much.

If you choose to go with the 'latest posts' option for your homepage (as is typical for blogs), then it will always be changing, showing your very latest post at the top of it.

WordPress themes have evolved, and one of my favourite features of the Genesis theme is the way it handles the homepage. The Genesis framework was the first template system I found that allowed us to create a homepage using widgets. You should be familiar with widgets by now, but if not, just think of them as user-definable areas where you can insert whatever you want.

The Genesis child themes do differ in the number and location of widgetized areas on the homepage, so you would need to check them out before buying one.

For example, the Genesis Lifestyle theme gives you three widgetized areas in addition to the usual header, sidebars and footers. You have 'Home', 'Home left' and 'Home right' and these are positioned directly where the main content of the homepage will go.

Here are those three widget areas:

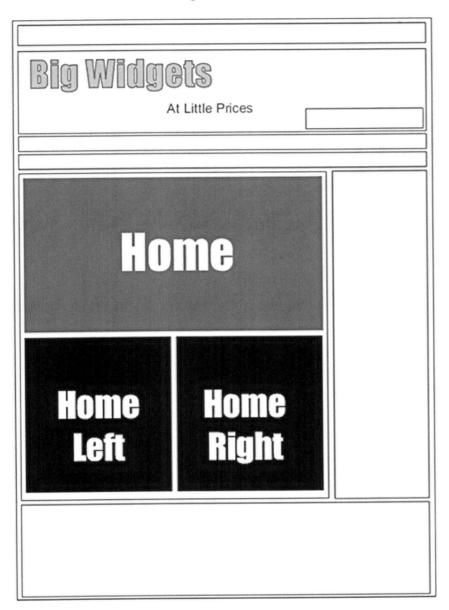

Those three widget areas can contain posts, pages, or just about anything else.

You can see this theme in action on the Lifestyle demo theme site:

http://demo.studiopress.com/lifestyle/

By contrast, the Genesis Balance theme has two homepage widget areas called 'Home Featured Left' and 'Home Featured Right'.

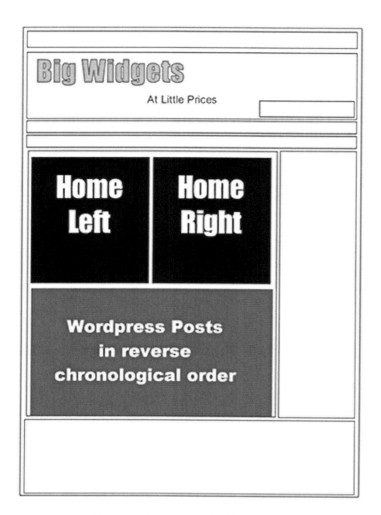

Under the 'home featured left' and 'home featured right' areas of the homepage, the normal WordPress loop is used to show the latest posts in reverse chronological order. You can also check out the Balance theme demo site to see how these widgetized areas were designed to work:

http://demo.studiopress.com/balance/

The two boxes at the top of that demo site are controlled by these two widgets.

I love the Genesis child themes because they give me so much scope for designing a homepage the way I want it to appear. The idea of using widgets for the homepage, wherever it came from, is pure genius.

18.1. Genesis Homepage Widgets

Genesis Framework comes with some really nice widgets that can help you create a great looking homepage (although these widgets can be used in any widgetized area, not just the homepage). Here are the ones that come pre-installed with Genesis:

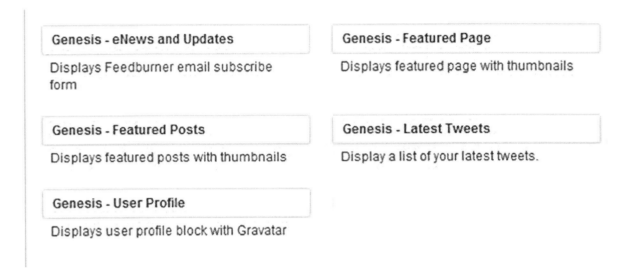

For some reason, two of those widgets have been depreciated, and when you try to install them, you are told to download and install different ones. I'll show you which they are as we go through them.

18.1.1. Genesis – eNews and Updates

This is one that has been depreciated. When you add it to a widgetized area, you'll see a link in the widget setup to download the 'Genesis eNews Extended' widget.

One of the important aspects of modern SEO is the need to keep visitors happy, and keep them coming back. This plugin allows you to insert an email-capture form on your site.

A good place to add this is at the top of the sidebar. If you are using a template like the Genesis Balance child theme, then this would go nicely in the top widgetized area of the homepage. Having your sign-up form as one of the first things a visitor sees on arriving at your site is a smart move, providing that page makes a good first impression of course.

When the plugin is installed, you'll find the new widget in the widgets area of the Dashboard. On adding the widget, you can enter a FeedBurner ID to get the form to link to a FeedBurner account (this is so that people are notified when new content is added to your site), or you can set it up to work with your mailing list provider.

If you want to set this up, see the instructions that come with the plugin/widget.

18.1.2. Genesis – Featured Page

This is one of my favourite widgets for the homepage. It allows you to add a featured

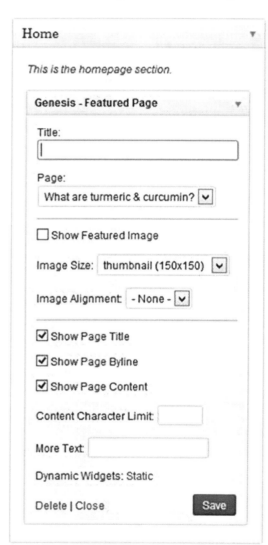

post to it. I typically add a featured page to the top of my homepage and then use other widgets below it that to fill out the page.

From an SEO perspective, if you add a complete featured post to the homepage, then you will not want the same post indexed on the post's own page (remember how WordPress duplicates the content?). There are two options that I have used on my sites.

1. Go in and set the page to noindex, follow (done from the 'Advance' tab of the WordPress SEO by Yoast plugin), so that the only copy of that article Google will know about, and therefore index, is the one on the homepage.

2. Use the <!—more--> tag to limit how much of the page is shown on the homepage. I cover this in the next section of the book. I typically just show the first paragraph, which is usually a good introduction to the content.

If I use a featured page at the top of my homepage, it will be a page I setup which basically introduces the whole site and the concept of the project. When I first construct the site, I'll set that page as my homepage (see above). As I begin to add posts, I'll switch to showing only the first paragraph of the page (using the more quicktag), in one of these widgets, and then display post excerpts underneath.

In the screenshot above, you see that the widget can be configured to show the featured image, page title, byline & content. You can also limit the number of

88

characters of the content that are displayed. However, I recommend you use the more quicktag for that, as you'll be able to display *exactly* what you want, whereas the former option might cut off the excerpt mid-sentence.

18.1.3. Genesis – Featured Posts

This widget is similar to the 'Featured Page' widget, except this one displays a number of posts instead. On the Genesis themes, where you have 'home left' and 'home right' widget areas, I typically add featured posts widgets to these underneath my featured post widget (in the Home widget area). That way I have the following layout on the homepage:

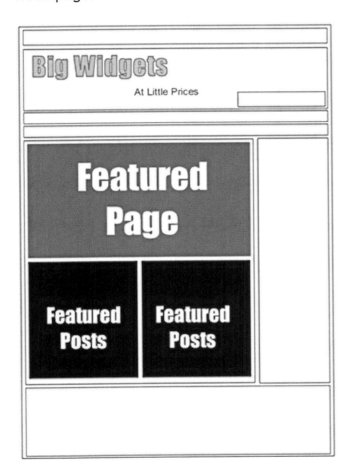

Using the featured posts widget is easy. Simply drag and drop it into the widgetized area and you'll get a stack of options:

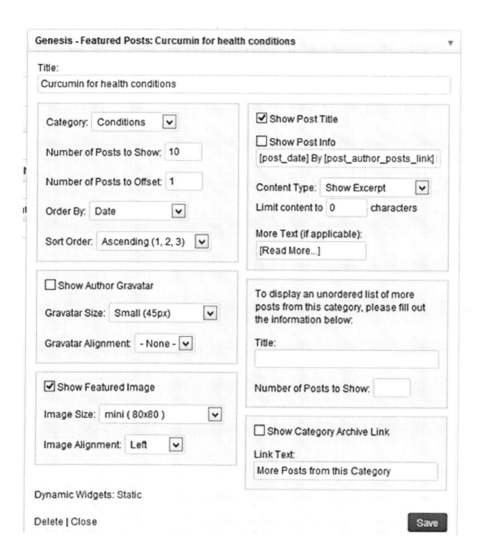

You can select which category you want to pull posts from, how many posts to show, and you can even offset the posts, for example, to skip the first X number of posts.

There are a number of reasons why you might want to offset the posts. One is if you are using two of these widgets to display posts from the same category. You might show the first five in one widget, and then in the second widget, you need to offset it by '5' so that the same five don't show up.

I often have mine offset by '1' if I am using a non-Genesis theme. This is because the first post in all of my categories is an 'announcement' post, created by the WP-Sticky WordPress plugin. You'll see why later in the book, when I show you how to set up category pages.

Other possibilities with the featured posts widget include how you order the posts, whether a featured image is shown next to them, plus other options. This plugin is highly customizable, and one of the most useful I've seen for constructing a homepage.

For SEO purposes, I recommend you set the widget to 'Show Excerpts' for each post. We'll look at how to add excerpts to a post later in the book. If you forget to add an excerpt to a post, the plugin will use the opening text in the article as its description.

18.1.4. Genesis – Latest Tweets

This is another widget that is depreciated. When you add it to a widgetized area, you will be asked to install a different plugin. The widget allows you to add an element to your site that shows your recent tweets on Twitter. If you make use of Twitter, that can be a good feature as it will encourage people to follow you (that's assuming they like what they see in the stream displayed on your site).

I will just mention that this plugin does seem to stop working at times, so do make sure it is functional if add it to your site.

18.1.5. Genesis – User Profile

As I've mentioned previously, people like to deal with 'real' people. This widget allows you to add your photo and short bio to your website. I usually add mine in the footer area:

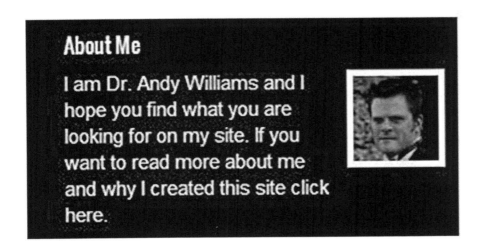

You have a few options with this widget:

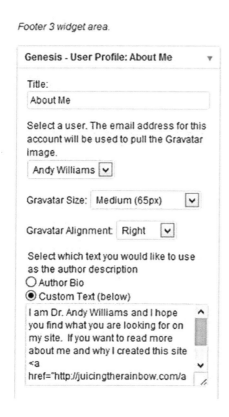

Give the widget a title, select your user profile, and choose the preferred alignment and size of the image. You can then use the bio you setup earlier in your user profile, or you can add custom text if you want (which is what I have done in my screenshot).

There are a couple of other options with this widget:

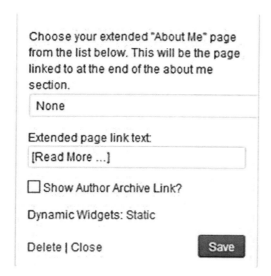

For example, you can specify a page on your site with a more complete bio. This will then be linked to at the end of the 'About Me' section.

You can also include a link to your author archive on the site (which I don't really recommend as the author archive page is not very user friendly to be honest).

By using these widgets, you can create a homepage that links to the most important pages on your site, and that's good for both SEO and your visitors.

18.2. The <!--more--> Quicktag

When you insert the <!--more--> quicktag into the text of a post, it will break the post at that exact point, and only display the text above the tag. There will be a 'read more' link at the point of the break, so people can click on that and be taken to the full article.

While this quicktag can be used for any post on your site, I like to use it on posts appearing on the homepage in order to stop full piece from being displayed. This helps to reduce duplication on the site.

Here is an example on my ezSEONews.com website.

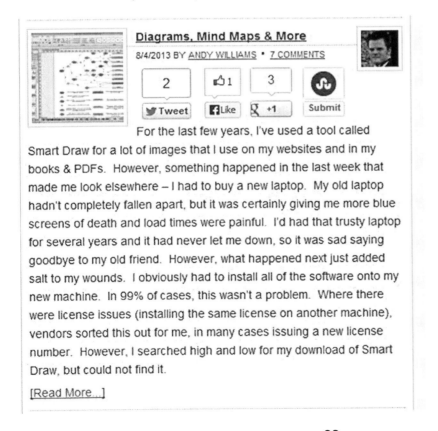

Diagrams, Mind Maps & More

8/4/2013 BY ANDY WILLIAMS • 7 COMMENTS

2   👍1   3

🐦Tweet   📘Like   🔴+1   Submit

For the last few years, I've used a tool called Smart Draw for a lot of images that I use on my websites and in my books & PDFs. However, something happened in the last week that made me look elsewhere – I had to buy a new laptop. My old laptop hadn't completely fallen apart, but it was certainly giving me more blue screens of death and load times were painful. I'd had that trusty laptop for several years and it had never let me down, so it was sad saying goodbye to my old friend. However, what happened next just added salt to my wounds. I obviously had to install all of the software onto my new machine. In 99% of cases, this wasn't a problem. Where there were license issues (installing the same license on another machine), vendors sorted this out for me, in many cases issuing a new license number. However, I searched high and low for my download of Smart Draw, but could not find it.

[Read More...]

See where it says 'Read More'? That is the position of the 'more tag' in my article. Here it is in the post editor:

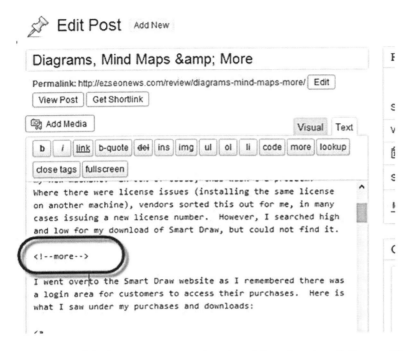

NOTE: Add the more tag in the 'Text' tab of the editor.

When using this 'more' quicktag, we have another method of adding an introduction to an article, and a link to read the whole piece on its own 'post' page. We just select the first paragraph of the post, add a more tag after it, and it's done.

Note that when you use this 'more tag', and have an excerpt created for a particular post, the more tag will be used on the homepage, author page, category page and tag page, while the excerpt will be used on the search page, plus some areas controlled by plugins, such as the related post, recent posts, and so on.

18.3. "Nofollow" Links

This isn't just an attribute to be used on homepages; it is a concern for all posts and pages on your entire site.

The nofollow tag can be added to any link to stop the search engines from following it.

Here is an example link with the nofollow attribute assigned to it:

<a href="http://google.com" **rel="nofollow"**>Google</a>

It's a good idea to nofollow links on your site that you don't want to waste link juice on. These include the legal pages (contact, privacy, etc). We've already seen this earlier in the book when we setup the legal menu to automatically nofollow the links.

I'd also recommend you nofollow *all* affiliate links.

When you are writing content that links to another authority website, do NOT add nofollow. We want Google to know we endorse these other credible sites by leaving the nofollow off the link.

These guidelines go for all pages on your site, and not just the homepage.

18.4. Getting Social on Your Site

It is a good idea to include ways for your visitors to follow you on various social channels that you use, e.g. Twitter, Facebook & Google plus, to name but three. A great widget that can add this to your site is the '**Social Sticker**' that I mentioned in the plugin section. This will add buttons to your posts that visitors can click on to follow you on social media. Here is an example:

The plugin can easily add buttons like this to your site's sidebar, included on *every* web page of your site, and not just the homepage.

Google are certainly paying a lot more attention to social shares as ranking signals, so you will also want to have a social sharing plugin installed for adding buttons to every post on the site like the one below:

KD Suite review

17/6/2013 BY <u>ANDY WILLIAMS</u> • <u>21 COMMENTS</u> <u>(EDIT)</u>

Back in July 2012, I started publishing on Amazon Kindle using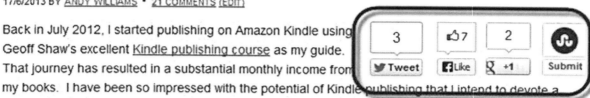
Geoff Shaw's excellent <u>Kindle publishing course</u> as my guide.
That journey has resulted in a substantial monthly income from
my books. I have been so impressed with the potential of Kindle publishing that I intend to devote a
bigger chunk of my own time to this market. I had even considered writing a piece of software to help me
decide on the best books to write (i.e. those with big markets that are selling well in Kindle). However,
last week I saw an email promotion for something called the <u>KD Suite</u>. I went to watch the video on the
sales page and immediately bought it. I've been playing with it ever since and I love it.

19. SEO When Writing Content

In this section, I just want to highlight a few points about writing content and SEO, plus mention the specific features you can use to help with the Search Engine Optimisation on your WordPress pages and WordPress posts.

With any type of content, posts or pages, it is important to follow a few general rules to ensure you do not fall foul of Google's Panda or Penguin algorithm. In the old days of SEO (pre-2011), webmasters tried to rank specifically for a keyword phrase or two, and would insert the exact phrase in a number of places like the title, filename, H1 header, opening paragraph, closing paragraph, ALT tags, and also worked into various other paragraphs within the article body too. Today that is just asking for trouble. The era of targeting specific words and phrases are just about over.

The best approach to writing good quality content is to write for your visitor, and not the search engines. If you right naturally, and with a sound knowledge of the topic, you will automatically include relevant words and phrases into your content anyway, which will help it rank for a whole host of search phrases. By all means include a specific phrase somewhere, such as the title or H1 header, but don't, whatever you do, start stuffing the same phrase in as many places as possible. Google are clever enough now to know what the page is about, even without strategic keyword placements by the webmaster. Concentrate on providing great quality content that will please your visitors, and that Google will want to rank highly because it deserves to.

With that in mind, create a compelling headline for your post, and don't try to stuff it with individual keywords or keyword phrases either. Just aim to create quality content, and forget about trying to optimise it for any specific words or phrases.

Tip: If you read your content out loud, and it sounds unnatural because of keywords that have been forced into the text, then it's not great content.

Another thing to think about is the 'slug' of your post or page. The slug is the filename, and it is automatically generated by WordPress when you publish content. WordPress takes your content's title, replaces spaces with dashes, removes any non-alphanumeric characters, and uses that (see below):

In the screenshot above, the title of the article is 'curcumin for weight loss'. The slug that WordPress created is **curcumin-for-weight-loss**.

You can change the slug if you want to; perhaps if there's a better way of naming it, or maybe the title of your article is long (it's a good idea to keep your URLs short). To edit the slug, click the '**Edit**' button next to the permalink URL at the top of your post/page, and then modify it to what you want. Finally, make sure you Publish/Update your page to save the changes.

19.1. SEO for WordPress Pages

The first thing I should mention about WordPress pages is that they can now have comments. This wasn't always the case, but I guess WordPress caved in to popular demand (of those that used pages for content when they should have perhaps used posts!).

Discussion

☐ Allow comments.
☐ Allow trackbacks and pingbacks on this page.

The way we are using WordPress pages (for legal pages), it's unlikely you'll want to enable that option. We don't particularly want people commenting on our privacy policy or contact pages! However, if you do have a page that you would like to enable comments on, this is where you do it on a page-by-page basis (the Discussion box is located below the text editor). If you don't see it, check the screen options (top right of the Dashboard).

Fortunately, a lot of the SEO we control on pages (and posts), is supplied to us by the Yoast WordPress SEO plugin. You'll find a section created by this plugin as you scroll down the page edit screen. It's typically located just under the text editor:

WordPress SEO by Yoast

General | Page Analysis Advanced Social

Snippet Preview:

Focus Keyword: (?)

SEO Title: (?)

Title display in search engines is limited to 70 chars, 20 chars left.

Meta Description: (?)

The meta description will be limited to 156 chars, 156 chars left.

There are 4 tabs across the top of this plugin. The first is the '**General**' tab. This shows a preview of what your listing is likely to look like in Google, with Title, URL and Description.

Below the '**Snippet Preview:**' there is a box labelled '**Focus Keyword**'. I would leave this empty and not use this feature of the plugin. When on-page SEO was all about optimizing for a specific keyword phrase, this plugin helped to make sure that phrase was found in all of the important parts of the page (title, header, article, etc). This is a dangerous procedure these days, so I recommend you do NOT use this plugin's on-page optimisation features.

There are also boxes for an SEO Title and Meta Description. If you are unhappy with the title WordPress created for you (possibly with the help of the Yoast WordPress SEO plugin, as you'll see later in the book), you can create your own title that will be used when the page is rendered.

The Meta Description box allows you to create a unique Meta Description tag for your page. If the page is one that you hope people will visit through the search engines, then add a good description here; otherwise leave it blank and Google will create a description for your page from its content.

The '**Page Analysis**' tab of this plugin is used to help optimize the page around your focus keyword. We aren't using this, so ignore this tab altogether.

On the 'Advanced' tab, there are some really useful features:

| General | Page Analysis | Advanced | Social |

Meta Robots Index: Default for post type, currently: index ▾

Meta Robots Follow: ⦿ Follow ◯ Nofollow

Meta Robots Advanced:
```
None          ^
NO ODP
NO YDIR
No Archive
No Snippet     v
```
Advanced meta robots settings for this page.

Include in HTML Sitemap: Auto detect ▾
Should this page be in the HTML Sitemap at all times, regardless of Robots Meta settings?

Canonical URL:
The canonical URL that this page should point to, leave empty to default to permalink. Cross don supported too.

301 Redirect:
The URL that this page should redirect to.

At the top, you have the option of controlling search engine robot commands for the page.

The '**Meta Robots Index:**' dropdown box is set to allow spiders to index the page by default. You can, however, set this to 'noindex' if it is a page you don't want the search engines to include in their search results.

I recommend you set *all* your legal pages to 'noindex'.

Under this box is the '**Meta Robots Follow:**' from where you can specify whether you want links on the page followed or nofollowed. I recommend you leave this to follow for *all* pages, since we want links on the page to be followed in order to help the site's indexing.

Next we have the '**Meta Robots Advanced:**' options. You can set a few preferences here. The only time you really need to change this from the default of 'None', is when you don't want a page archived in the search engines. Again, I recommend this for *all* legal pages as this will prevent Google from retaining a cached version of them.

Now we have the 'Include in HTML Sitemap:' option. Here we can specify whether or not we want the page to appear in the sitemap that Yoast's WordPress SEO plugin creates. For legal pages, I would select 'Never include'. For everything else, leave it at the default setting of 'Auto Detect'.

The next box allows you to specify a 'Canonical URL:' for the page. You should not have to bother with this option as WordPress looks after it for us.

The '301 Redirect:' option allows you to enter a URL that this page should automatically redirect to. That is, when someone loads the page, it redirects to the URL you enter here. 301 redirects are typically used to notify the search engines that a page or post has permanently moved to a new URL. For example, if you had a page that had a lot of links pointing to it, but you wanted to move that page to a new URL - for whatever reason - you could 301 the original to the new, and all those links would still count to towards the ranking of the new page URL.

On the 'Social' tab, you can enter a custom description for the page so that if someone shares it on Facebook or Google+, this description will be used instead of the default one.

OK, that's the Yoast WordPress settings for WordPress pages. Let's now look at SEO on WordPress posts.

19.2. SEO for WordPress Posts

WordPress posts have a few more SEO options than WordPress pages. We still have the Yoast WordPress SEO plugin options that we saw in the previous section on 'WordPress Pages', and they are used in exactly the same way. If you need to noindex, follow a post (as we will do later when we look at setting up category pages), then you do it using the '**Advanced**' tab of that plugin's options.

Also, you will notice that if you go to **Posts -> All Posts**, in the WordPress Dashboard, there are a few extra columns tacked on to the end of the table:

I would suggest you ignore these columns, as they are part of the keyword optimisation features in the plugin. Remember I advised you earlier not to use those features as they are likely to hurt, rather than help, your site's rankings).

19.2.1. Post Categories
One of the benefits of using posts for publishing your main, visitor-orientated content is that you can group them into categories. These act as organised 'silos' of content, all related to the core topic. When you add a post, you can select the category from a list of those which you have already set up.

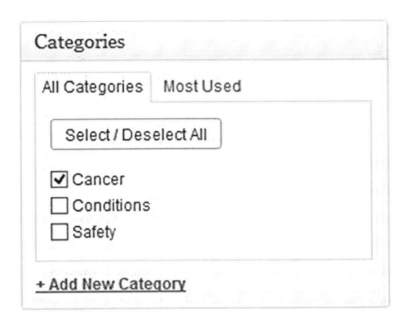

From an SEO point of view, it is better to only have posts in ONE category. If you find that you need to categorise a post into multiple categories, then you probably don't have the correct categories in the first place. Categories should be broad enough so that there isn't much, or any, overlap. If you find that you want to further classify your posts, look at using tags instead. We'll be looking more into tags later in the book.

There are a few reasons why one post for one category is a good idea.

Firstly, if you put a post in three categories, then three copies of that post will be created (one on each category page), though we will largely overcome this problem later when setting up the category pages. A more important reason for the one post one category rule is the SEO benefit. We want categories to contain tightly focused groups of content. Using a plugin like YARPP (see the plugins section of this book for details), we can setup a 'Related Posts' section for every post on the site. These related links (or excerpts with links to the related posts), show other posts within the same category. Therefore related posts are interlinking with each other, and that will help boost your rankings. This is because Google likes it when a post has links from related content. Another SEO benefit comes from the category pages. These pages link out to highly related articles on the site, so once again, the relevancy factors of links to-and-from related content is a big on-page SEO advantage.

19.2.2. Post Tags

Tags are an additional way to categorize your content. When you add a post, you can enter one or more tags for it:

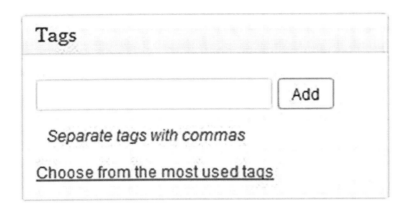

You simply enter them, with each tag separated by a comma.

For every tag you enter, WordPress creates a separate webpage that lists all posts using that tag. As you can imagine, duplicate content is an issue again. When a site uses tags incorrectly, major SEO problems arise. For example, I've seen websites that have dozens of tags per post. In many cases, a tag might only be used ONCE on the entire site. That means the tag page will contain one article. What is the point of that tag page, since the article already appears on its own post webpage?

The purpose of tags is similar to the purpose of categories. It's used to assemble related content into related groups so that visitors (and search engines), can find information more easily.

For example, suppose you had a website about Huskies with lots of content, videos, and photos. You could setup categories like grooming, feed, training, etc. You might also like to categorise your posts according to whether they were articles, photos or videos. You might then use the tags: articles, photos, videos. Some pieces of content would include two, or even all three of these tags, and that is fine. We do still end up with duplication issues because the same article may then be posted on two or three tag pages. However, we'll look later at how we can minimise this duplication issue and add more value to tag pages.

The benefit of the tag pages is that it adds an extra level of categorisation which the visitor will find useful (if done properly). So, someone looking for images of Huskies can visit the 'photo' tag page, and find all the pictures listed together on there. It's the same principle for those looking for videos or content, etc.

From a search engine point of view, tag pages do tend to rank well because multiple posts typically point at each tag page. Later in the book, we'll look at how we can modify these tag pages to offer our visitors, and the search engines, even more worth.

My two suggestions for using tags is to only use those that appear (or will appear), on multiple posts of the site, and that you limit the number of tags per post to a maximum of four or five.

19.2.3. Post Formatting

At the top of the WYSIWYG (What-You-See-Is-What-You-Get), editor on the edit post screen is the toolbar.

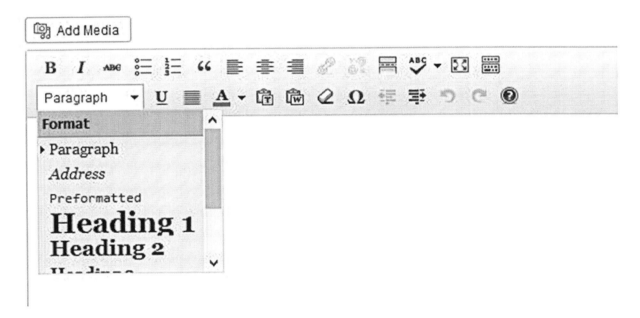

By default, the toolbar only contains the top row of buttons. To show the bottom row of tool buttons (which includes the important text formatting dropdown box), you have to click the button on the far right of the top toolbar. That button toggles between top only, and both toolbars.

Note: With formatting comes great responsibility.

With formatting options, like bold, underline & italics, only use them where you would if search engines did not exist. What I mean by that is do not be tempted to put bold or italics on the words and phrases you want to rank for. This might have worked a few years ago, but today it's a signal to Google that you are trying to over-optimise your page for those words and phrases. SEO on your page should be 'invisible', meaning it should not be obvious what you are trying to rank for when reading the content.

For headers, only include one 'Heading 1' headline per page (this uses the H1 HTML tag). Your template is likely to use an H1 for the title of the post, so you shouldn't add a second H1 header. Use headlines in hierarchies, with an H2 being the start of a new section, and H3 as sub-sections of the H2. If you then start a new section, use another H2.

Again, as with all areas of your content, do not stuff keyword phrases into headlines because they'll do you NO favours.

We've already discussed the extra features that the Yoast WordPress SEO plugin adds to post and page edit screens, and how you can use them to change the Title or Meta Description of your page or post. Therefore we won't go into that again. Instead, let's move on to excerpts.

19.3. Optimizing Images Used in Posts

The '**Add Media**' button above the toolbar, allows you to insert images and other media into your posts and pages. For images used in posts, I would recommend you optimize them as follows:

- Try to compress the image to as small a size as possible before uploading. Remember that when someone visits your page, the images have to download to their computers, thus slowing page load times.
- Keep image file size small, and resize images to the correct size (dimensions) before uploading. For example, if your theme content area is 600 pixels, and you want the image to take up half the width of the content, resize the image so that it is 300 pixels wide.
- Give your image a name that best describes it. Once again, remember not to keyword stuff here, and don't use words and phrases that are irrelevant to the image.
- Use ALT tags for all your images, and I say again, don't keyword stuff. Describe the image appropriately so that blind or partially sighted users can understand your content.

19.4. Internal Linking Between Posts

The YARPP plugin we mentioned in the plugins section of this book will create 'related posts' sections on each of your posts if you want them there. That helps to interlink your related content and spread link juice around your site. One of the more powerful 'on-page techniques' is to link words and phrases in one post to another 'related post', though you shouldn't do this just for the sake of internal linking.

Let me give you an example of how this is used for maximum SEO benefit.

Suppose you had an article called 'World's Best Hot Dog Recipe', and in that article you mention a special tomato sauce that you make for your hot dogs. On your site somewhere you have shared that recipe. Therefore, in the hot dog article, when you mention the special sauce, you link to that post on your site. Internal linking like this is natural, helps visitors, and is a powerful SEO tool to help our pages rank better.

I did an experiment with internal linking on one of my sites. I described the experiment and results here:

http://ezseonews.com/backlinks/internal-linking-seo/

19.5. Featured Images for Posts

Posts can be assigned a featured image, which is used to show up next to the post wherever it is listed on your site. Whether you use them or not depends on how you want your site to look. Personally I think they help break up blocks of text on a webpage, therefore helping the visitor to navigate to stuff easier.

If you do use them, make sure you follow the image optimization tips above for these as well. Remember, if you have a list of say 20 posts on a page, with 20 featured images, they are going to slow the page load time considerably. Optimizing these images as best you can, both in size (KB), and dimensions (pixels), will help to improve page load speeds.

19.6. Post Excerpts

Excerpts are short summaries of your post. Think of them in the same way as you think of a Meta Description. It should be something short and enticing to the visitor. Remember, these extracts will be displayed on various areas of your website serving as descriptions for the posts.

Excerpt

Excerpts are optional hand-crafted summaries of your content that can be used in your theme. Learn more about manual excerpts.

If you don't see this section, check the Screen Options (top right of the WordPress Dashboard).

Excerpts have to main purposes:

1. To add a description to the posts in your RSS feeds.
2. To supply summaries to posts in various areas of your site, like search results, tag & category pages, author pages, etc. (depending on the theme you are using).

Excerpts may also be used as the Meta Description tag with some themes.

A good reason to use excerpts is that they provide complete descriptions for any post. If you don't have excerpts written for a post, then WordPress will create a description based on the content of your page, and that will usually stop mid-word or mid-sentence.

I therefore recommend writing an excerpt for *all* posts on your site.

19.7. Allow Comments & Trackbacks on Posts?

You can enable or disable comments and trackbacks on posts if you want to, either globally or on a post -by-post basis. I recommend you keep comments enabled on all posts, because social interaction is an important aspect of our SEO efforts.

Trackbacks are a little more difficult to give a hard and fast rule about. Essentially, a trackback is like a comment sent to your site from another site, when that other site links to yours. While it is nice to know who is linking to us, this feature has been heavily abused by spammers. This means that 99% of the time, a trackback is bogus and no link exists. The reason the spammers do this is to try to get you to approve their 'trackback', which then goes live on your site with a link back to theirs. I tend to turn trackbacks off on all posts by default because spammers were taking up too much of my time; constantly checking to see if a site had really linked to mine or not. Don't forget, you can choose whether to enable or disable globally, or on a post by post basis.

19.8. Scheduling Posts

There may be times when you want to schedule posts into the future. For example, if I am adding 10-20 posts to my site (let's say I just got a bunch of content from my ghost writer), I would schedule those posts to be released over 2-3 weeks. Doing this encourages the search engine spiders to come back more regularly. It can also incite visitors to return more often when they see that fresh content is being added frequently.

To schedule posts, look to the 'Publish' section located on the right of the post edit screen:

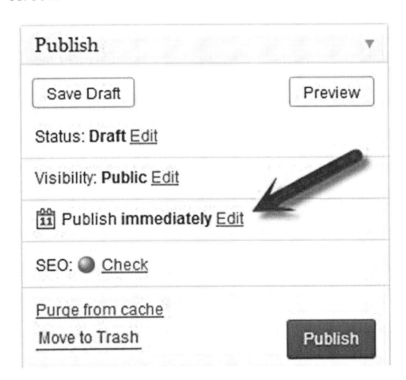

Where it says '**Publish immediately**', there is an '**Edit**' link that allows you to change the date and time of publication. The edit link expands the area:

Now you can select a date, and even a time, for when the article will be published. When that date and time arrives, WordPress automatically publishes the article for you. You do not have to login or do anything else once this is set up.

20. Setting up Category Pages

Categories are used to classify posts, and WordPress will create 'category pages' which list all posts within that category. This helps visitors and search engines alike.

When you setup a category on your site, I highly recommend you give your new category a description.

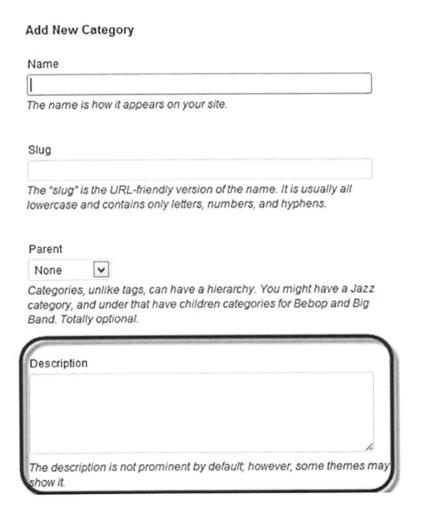

These descriptions are used as mouse-over hints if you are using a category widget in your sidebar.

It's the little things that make the biggest difference, and small details like this help guide your visitors, and therefore make your site stand out from the vast majority that don't bother with such features. It is also worth mentioning that the text you enter for the description will appear in the code of your web page (as a Title Tag in the URL of the category link), and Google obviously sees that.

OK, let's leave the setting up of categories, and turn our attention to category pages. This is where I do things a little differently from most others.

20.1. A Typical Category Page

A typical WordPress category page will just list all of the posts in that category. It will look something like this:

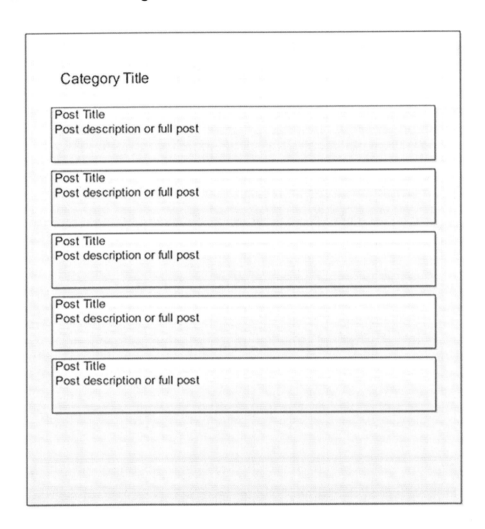

Depending on the theme you are using, those posts may be showing as title with excerpt, or title with full post. Obviously the latter would cause huge duplication problems since these category pages would contain the complete text of all posts within the category.

If this is what your category pages look like, then you should *noindex, follow* the category pages. We can easily do this thanks to the WordPress SEO plugin (located under the text editor in the WordPress Dashboard).

NOTE: The SEO plugin allows you to treat entities globally, or on a one-by-one basis. Therefore you can globally set all category pages to *noindex, follow*, or you can set just one or two category pages to *noindex, follow*. The same goes for tag pages, posts, pages, etc.

20.1.1. Globally Set All Category Pages to Noindex, Follow

To make *all* category page *noindex, follow*, go to the **SEO -> Titles & Metas** section, and click on the '**Taxonomies**' tab.

Categories

Title template:	%%term_title%% Archives %%page%% %%sep%% %%sitename%%
Meta description template:	
Meta Robots:	☐ noindex, follow
WordPress SEO Meta Box:	☐ Hide

Simply check the '**Meta Robots**' check box, and all category pages will become *noindex, follow*. This means search engine robots can find the category pages and follow links on them, but it won't index and include them in the search results.

20.1.2. Setting Individual Category Pages to Noindex, Follow

To make category pages *noindex, follow* on a one-by-one basis, you need to go to the **Posts -> Categories** section of the Dashboard, and click on a category's '**Edit**' link for the one you want to modify.

Note: You need to create the category first, and then go in and edit it, because these extra options are not found on the main screen from where you create new categories.

When you go into the category edit screen, there are a number of new options available to you thanks to Yoast's WordPress SEO plugin.

Yoast WordPress SEO Settings

SEO Title:

The SEO title is used on the archive page for this term.

SEO Description:

The SEO description is used for the meta description on the archive page for this term.

Canonical:

The canonical link is shown on the archive page for this term.

Breadcrumbs Title:

The Breadcrumbs title is used in the breadcrumbs where this category appears.

Noindex this category: `Use category default (Currently: index)` ⌄

Include in sitemap?: `Auto detect` ⌄

These options allow us override any or all of the global category settings. On a one-by-one basis, we can define a custom Title and Description, make the category page *noindex, follow*, and exclude it from the sitemap.

NOTE: If you *noindex, follow,* your category pages, I don't recommend excluding the category pages from the sitemap. Google will find the category pages in the sitemap and then spider them to find all of your content. But Google won't index and rank these pages, which is what we want.

20.2. A Better Category Page?

Instead of just listing posts within a category, wouldn't it be better if our category pages looked like this:

```
┌─────────────────────────────────────────────────┐
│                                                 │
│   Category Title                                │
│   ┌─────────────────────────────────────────┐   │
│   │ Introduction to category page           │   │
│   │ Introductory article                    │   │
│   │                                         │   │
│   │                                         │   │
│   │                                         │   │
│   │                                         │   │
│   │                                         │   │
│   │                                         │   │
│   │                                         │   │
│   └─────────────────────────────────────────┘   │
│   ┌─────────────────────────────────────────┐   │
│   │ Post Title                              │   │
│   │ Post excerpt                            │   │
│   └─────────────────────────────────────────┘   │
│   ┌─────────────────────────────────────────┐   │
│   │ Post Title                              │   │
│   │ Post excerpt                            │   │
│   └─────────────────────────────────────────┘   │
│   ┌─────────────────────────────────────────┐   │
│   │ Post Title                              │   │
│   │ Post excerpt                            │   │
│   └─────────────────────────────────────────┘   │
│                                                 │
└─────────────────────────────────────────────────┘
```

In this category page, there is a text introduction to the category, followed by post Titles and post Excerpts of all the articles within the category.

The written introduction adds SEO benefits, in that this page now has some unique content on it, and introduces the posts in the category to both my visitors and the search engines. I typically add this type of introduction to *all* of my category pages, and then leave them as *index, follow*. This is because I want the search engines to index and rank my category pages when they're set up in this way.

20.2.1. For Genesis Users

The Genesis theme has some features built in that allow you to add this type of introduction to both category pages, and tag pages. I love the fact that Genesis has built this into their theme because it makes things that much easier.

Early Genesis versions were a little buggy with formatting and line-spacing issues. However, with the latest versions of Genesis, this feature seems to work well. And while you cannot create formatted text with a WYSIWYG editor, if you know some basic HTML, you can use it in the descriptions without any problems.

If you are using Genesis, and you want to check out these features, go back to the Posts -> Categories edit page, and you'll see the following (underneath the Yoast category settings):

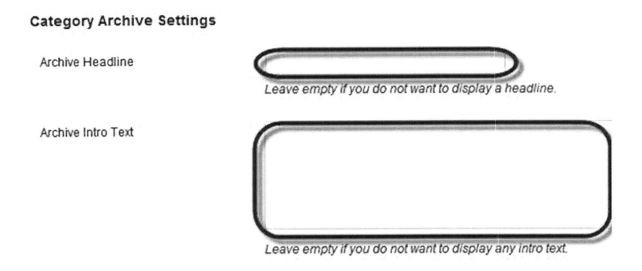

Here you can add both a headline and introductory text.

This will then be fixed at the top of the category page before the posts are shown. You then need to make sure that only the title and excerpts of posts are displayed, and you can do that in the **Genesis -> Theme Settings**.

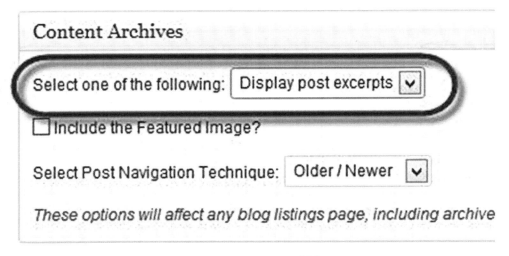

Change that drop down box in the 'Content Archives' section to 'Display post excerpts'.

That's all there is to it. Genesis users can use this built in feature to easily add unique introductory content to their category pages.

But what if you don't use Genesis? Well, you can use WP-Sticky, a plugin to help achieve a similar result.

20.2.2. Using WP-Sticky

While this method is not needed by Genesis users, I still use it on a lot of my sites because of the flexibility it offers.

The process is not perfect (see the note about hierarchical categories at the end), but it does allow you to use WordPress posts as introductions on category pages.

Since WordPress posts can include images, videos, text formatting, email capture forms, calls to action, and so on and so forth, your introductions can be anything you want them to be.

To use this feature, we need the plugin called WP Sticky. We mentioned it in the plugins section of the book, so go and install that if you haven't already done so.

Once installed, head on over to **Settings -> WP-Sticky**, and change the top option to yes:

Note: WP-Sticky allows us to permanently fix an article to the top of a category page. It works in a different way to the 'sticky' feature built into WordPress, so don't try to do this technique without the WP-Sticky plugin.

This is what we are going to do:

- Create a WordPress post to be used as an introduction to a category.
- Stick it to the top of that category page.
- Setup the category page to show one full post, followed by excerpts of all other posts. If you are using Genesis themes, I'll give you the instructions to set this up. If you are using a different theme, you'll need to contact their support desk to find out how and if this is possible. If it is not possible, simply revert to plan A, and *noindex, follow,* all category pages.
- Now *Noindex, follow,* the introduction post (no archive it too, and also remove it from the sitemap), so that the search engines do not index it. This is because we only want the full post displayed and indexed on the category page.

1 & 2. Creating the Post and sticking it to the top of the category

Once you have written the post that you'll be using for the introduction of a category, select the category for the post, that is, the one you want the post to introduce. Now look for the WP-Sticky options on the right hand side of the edit screen.

Post Sticky Status

- ● Announcement
- ○ Sticky
- ○ Normal

You want to save this post as an '**Announcement**'. This will permanently stick it to the top of the category page.

3. Setup WordPress to show one full post, then excerpts for *all* category pages

Genesis Users:

In order to get Genesis to do what we want, we need to create a new template file and upload it to the child theme folder.

In a text editor, type out the following code:

```php
<?php
remove_action('genesis_post_content', 'genesis_do_post_content');
add_action('genesis_post_content', 'custom_post_content');
function custom_post_content() {
    global $loop_counter;

    if( $loop_counter < 1 ) {
        the_content();
    }
    else {
        the_excerpt();
    }
}
require_once(PARENT_DIR . '/index.php');
?>
```

Now save the file as **archive.php** and upload it to the child theme folder.

Here it is in my Lifestyle child theme folder:

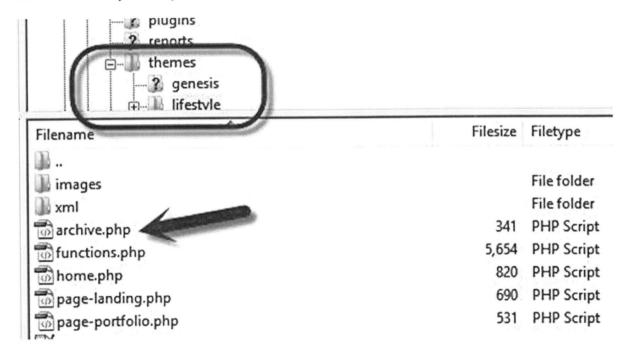

That's it! Your category pages should now show the first post as a full introductory post, followed by just the titles and excerpts of the remaining posts within those categories.

Non-Genesis Users

If you want to try to get this to work with a different theme, you may need to contact the theme's support and ask for help. Just tell them that you want the category pages on your site to show one full post, then the titles and excerpts of all remaining posts. They should be able to tell you if it's possible, and if yes, how to go about doing it.

4. Robot settings and sitemap exclusion

The final stage of this setup is to 'noindex', 'follow', the introductory post.

Just go in to edit the post as normal and use the Yoast WordPress SEO settings there to *noindex, and follow* it:

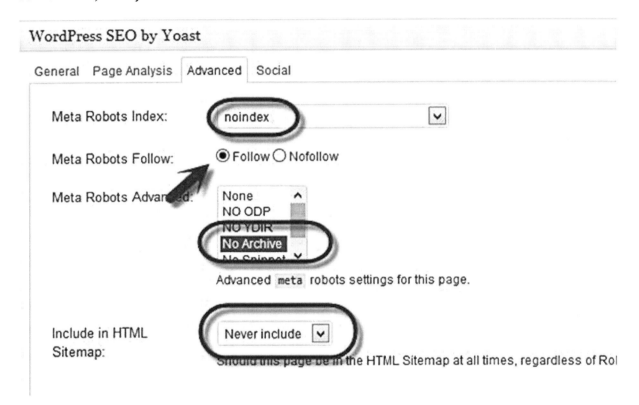

Set the **Meta Robots Index** value to **noindex**.

Set the **Meta Robots Follow** value to **Follow**.

Set the **Meta Robots Advanced** to **No Archive**.

Set **Include in HTML Sitemap** to **Never include**.

That's all there is to it. Your category page is now set up to show a full post first, then the titles and excerpts of all other posts in the category below that fixed intro.

A note about hierarchical categories

If you have categories with sub-categories, this technique won't work quite so well. It does work, but it's a little less controlled. You see, on the 'parent' category pages, after the fixed introduction post, the first few posts will always display the announcement posts created for the sub-categories, and then you'll get your remaining titles and excerpts.

This isn't an issue with Genesis users that opt for the built-in 'Intro Text' feature mentioned earlier.

21. Extending the SEO Value of Tag Pages

Tag pages can rank remarkably well because they tend to have a lot of internal links pointing at them (from all posts that use that tag). For this reason, I like to have these pages set as *index, follow*, but to be able to do this, we need to first modify the tag pages.

As we saw with the category setup in the previous chapter, Yoast's WordPress SEO plugin adds some extra features that allow us to better handle Category & Tag pages.

If you go and edit an existing tag (**Posts -> Tags**), you'll get the same Yoast settings we saw with the category pages, allowing you to create a custom Title and Description as well as being able to *noindex* a tag page and exclude it from the sitemap if you need to.

Inside the main **SEO -> Titles & Metas** settings, you can set the global rules for *all* tag pages, noindexing the lot if you want to.

NOTE: Like category pages, I don't recommend you exclude tag pages from the sitemap because they are useful to search engines for finding content on your site.

21.1. A Typical Tag Page

Again, just like the category pages, a typical WordPress tag page is just a list of all the posts on a site that have been tagged with a particular word or phrase. If this is what your tag pages are like, I recommend you **noindex,** and **follow** them in the global settings for tag pages.

21.2. A Better Kind of Tag Page

What I like to do is add an introduction to the tag pages in the same way that we handled the category pages.

Genesis Users

Fortunately for Genesis users, this is built into the theme like it is for the category pages.

Just login to your dashboard and go to **Posts -> Tags**. Click on the tag you want to add the introduction for, and you can then write the introductory text (just as we did for category pages).

Non-Genesis Users

For non-Genesis themes, you will need to ask your theme's support team if it is possible to add a fixed introduction to tag pages and then have all other posts display as titles and excerpts.

21.3. Tag Pages Summary

If you *can* set up your tag pages with introductions, then I recommend you globally set tag pages as *index, follow*, and add introductions to all tag pages.

If you cannot setup your tag pages to include an introduction, and then show all other posts as titles and excerpts, then I recommend you *noindex*, and *follow* all your tag pages. This is to prevent any potential duplicate content issues.

For those of you who want to implement intro text on tag and category pages, but don't use Genesis, you might be interested in this article on Yoast.com:

http://yoast.com/wordpress-archive-pages/

Just a word of warning though; you will need to play around with PHP code.

22. WordPress for SEO Plugin Setup

Yoast's WordPress plugin provides a massive amount of SEO control over your WordPress site. When you install it, you'll find SEO options popping up in several areas of your Dashboard. These areas can be divided into two main parts; those that control settings globally, and those that control settings on a one-by-one basis.

The 'Global' settings are found in the SEO menu of the WP Dashboard:

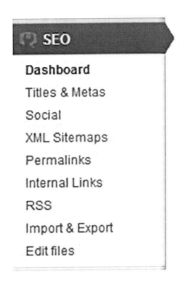

Changes made in here will affect all posts, all pages, all categories, and all tag pages, etc. However, we can override these settings on individual posts, pages, and categories etc.

For posts and pages, you'll find the override settings on the '**Edit Post**' and '**Edit Page**' screens. They look like this:

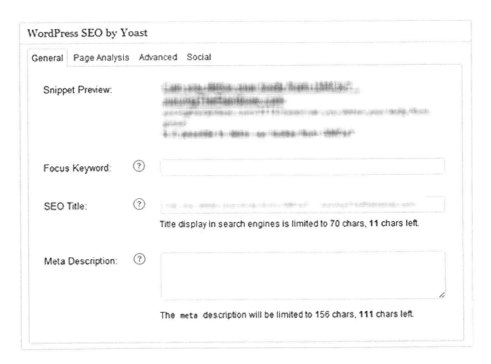

For Category and Tag page override settings, you go to the Posts -> Categories, or Posts -> Tags, respectively, and click on an item you want to edit. You'll then see the override settings for the individual category or tag page. Here are the override settings for a category:

Yoast WordPress SEO Settings

SEO Title:

Juicing can help with a number of diseases, either as a supporting

The SEO title is used on the archive page for this term.

SEO Description:

The SEO description is used for the meta description on the archive page for this term.

Canonical:

The canonical link is shown on the archive page for this term.

Breadcrumbs Title:

The Breadcrumbs title is used in the breadcrumbs where this category appears.

Noindex this category: Use category default (Currently: index) ▾

Include in sitemap?: Auto detect ▾

As you can see, you are able to set a different Title & Description, make the category index or noindex, and exclude from the sitemap if required. The Tag Page overrides are very similar to the Category ones.

OK, let's look at the '**Global Settings**'.

On the SEO -> Dashboard settings, you can click on the '**Start Tour**' button to learn more about the WordPress SEO plugin, and how it works. It will take you through the tabs of the plugin and show you basic information about the settings on each of those tabs.

There is nothing you need to set on this page of the plugin settings.

22.1. Title & Metas

The General tab

The '**Titles**' and '**Metas**' section has a lot of options, spread over several tabs.

On the 'General' tab, you should not need to change the 'Title Settings' checkbox at the top. The plugin has auto-detected whether this box should be checked or not and set it for you.

The only setting on this tab that I suggest you check is the '**Noindex subpages of archives**'. As archive pages fill up with posts, WordPress will create new pages to hold additional posts. This option prevents these additional pages from being indexed. The first page will still be indexed, and this is the important one for us.

There is a section on this settings page called '**Clean up the <head>**'. Basically WordPress has added a lot of code to the head section of your pages. These options allow you to remove them. However, I don't recommend you change any of these unless you understand *exactly* what they do. Just leave them all unchecked.

The Home tab

The Home tab allows you to specify '**templates**' for the homepage Title, homepage Meta Description and homepage Meta Keywords tags.

Note: If you do want to use the Meta Keywords tags but don't see the option, then go to the 'General Tab' and check the box that says: 'Use meta keywords tag?'

So what is a template? Well, if you click over to the '**Help**' tab of the '**Titles & Metas**' section, you can see a number of variables. These variables can be used to setup a template. So, for example, if we wanted the homepage title to include the site name, we could use the variable **%%sitename%%** in the template for the homepage.

The plugin would then pull the site's name from the WordPress settings and insert it wherever it sees the **%%sitename%%** variable.

So we could use a homepage Title like this:

%%sitename%% :: Making your dog happier

If your site name (in the WordPress General settings), was '**Doggy Treats**', then when the homepage was loaded in a browser, the homepage title would display as:

Doggy Treats :: Making your dog happier

We could of course use a variable to insert the tagline of the site into the title. This would do it:

%%sitename%% :: %%sitesdesc%%

The title would then pull the site name and tagline from the '**General Settings**' tab of your WP Dashboard, and create the title from those.

Now, you might ask why bother using variables for the homepage title when you can just type in the *exact title* you want. The main reason is in case you ever update the site title or tagline in your settings. By using variables, our titles will automatically get updated, without us having to remember to go in and manually change them.

The plugin sets the default homepage title as follows:

%%sitename%% %%page%% %%sep%% %%sitedesc%%

By looking at the variable list on the '**Help**' tab, you can decode this to see that the homepage title would be the site name, followed by a separator (**%%sep%%** - this is usually a dash, but that depends on the theme you are using), and then the site description (tagline). The **%%page%%** variable is not relevant to the homepage so it will be blank (I personally remove that variable from the homepage title template). Using our previous example, the title could therefore be:

Doggy Treats – Making your dog happier.

The default homepage title is OK and I would leave it as it is if I were you. For the description, you can use variables if you want, but I generally just type in my own description for the homepage.

The Post Types tab

The '**Post Types**' tab allows you to setup the default Title, Description, Keywords, and index status, etc., for posts, pages & media.

Since I like my websites to be '**branded**' by the site's name, I always include the **%%sitename%%** variable in the title of my posts, usually at the end of the title template. The one that is installed by default is actually quite good, because it uses the posts title and the site name. It also includes the **%%page%%** variable, which I would remove.

So my preferred title template for posts is.

%%title%% - %%sitename%%

For the post description, I use **%%excerpt%%**. This will then use whatever excerpt I have entered for a post as the Meta Description tag.

Here is my completed posts section:

Posts

Title template:	%%title%% - %%sitename%%
Meta description template:	%%excerpt%%
Meta keywords template:	
Meta Robots:	☐ noindex, follow
▸ Authorship:	☐ Don't show rel="author"
Date in Snippet Preview:	☐ Show date in snippet preview?
WordPress SEO Meta Box:	☐ Hide

By default, I have the '**Meta Robots**' disabled so that all of my posts are index, follow. All four of these boxes can be left unchecked.

For pages, I use the same title template as for posts. I leave the description box empty, since the pages on my site are the less important 'legal pages', that I noindex, and follow anyway. If I happen to want a page to specifically have a description, I can do that as I am creating it (and make that one page index, follow if I want to), using the Yoast SEO settings on the edit post screen to override these global settings. Here are my page settings:

Pages

Title template:	%%title%% - %%sitename%%
Meta description template:	
Meta keywords template:	
Meta Robots:	☑ noindex, follow
Authorship:	☐ Don't show rel="author"
Date in Snippet Preview:	☐ Show date in snippet preview?
WordPress SEO Meta Box:	☐ Hide

Notice that I have checked the noindex, follow box. This means that by default, all pages will be noindex, follow. Because of the way I use pages, I don't want them showing up in the search engines.

For media, these are special posts created by WordPress to hold information about the media you upload. I don't want mine indexed as separate pages, so here are the settings I use:

Media

Title template:	%%title%% - %%sitename%%
Meta description template:	%%caption%%
Meta keywords template:	
Meta Robots:	☑ noindex, follow
Authorship:	☐ Don't show rel="author"
Date in Snippet Preview:	☐ Show date in snippet preview?
WordPress SEO Meta Box:	☐ Hide

130

Again, the media settings use noindex, follow, because I don't want these files ending up in the search engines (I only want the posts that use these files to be indexed).

The Taxonomies tab

Under the 'Taxonomies tab', we can setup the global options for Categories, Tags, and Format.

Here are my settings for Categories:

Categories

Title template:	%%term_title%% on %%sitename%%
Meta description template:	%%category_description%%
Meta keywords template:	
Meta Robots:	☐ noindex, follow
WordPress SEO Meta Box:	☐ Hide

The **%%term_title%%** variable will be replaced by the category title and the **%%category_description%%** will be replaced by the description we entered for the category.

IMPORTANT: I have my category pages set globally to be indexed. That is because I set them up to include an introduction at the top, followed by post excerpts (See the category setup section of this book if you need to recap). If you do not use an introduction on your category pages, set the 'Meta Robots:' to noindex, follow.

Here are my Tags settings:

Tags

Title template:

> Articles about %%term_title%% on %%sitename%%

Meta description template:

> %%tag_description%%

Meta keywords template:

Meta Robots: ☐ noindex, follow

WordPress SEO Meta Box: ☐ Hide

Again, I have my tag pages set to be indexed. That is only because I have an introduction on all of my tag pages, followed by excerpts of the posts using that tag (see the tag page setup section of this book if you need to recap). If you do not have introductory text on your tag pages, set the 'Meta Robots:' to noindex, follow.

The Format options under the 'Taxonomies' tab can be left unchanged.

The Other tab

This tab allows us to set the global settings for author and date archives, search pages, and 404 pages.

Here are my settings for author archives:

Author Archives

Title template:

> %%name%% on %%sitename%%

Meta description template:

Meta keywords template:

Meta Robots: ☑ noindex, follow

☐ Disable the author archives

If you're running a one author blog, the author archive will always look exactly the same as your homepage. And even though you may not link to it, others might, to do you harm. Disabling them here will make sure any link to those archives will be 301 redirected to the homepage.

132

Note that for the 'Meta Robots:' I have noindex, follow checked. That is because I don't want the author archive pages to get into the search engines, as it would only add to the duplicate content problem. However, with this setting, Google can still follow the links on the page to help with the spidering of the site.

Since I have this set as noindex, there is no need to enter a Meta Description here.

For 'Date Archives', I use these settings:

Date Archives

Title template:

> %%sitename%% archives from %%date%%

Meta description template:

Meta Robots:

☑ noindex, follow

☐ Disable the date-based archives

For the date based archives, the same applies: they probably look a lot like your homepage, and could thus be seen as duplicate content.

Again, this is noindex, follow to reduce duplicate content in Google.

The last couple of options are for the 'Special Pages'. I use these settings:

Special Pages

These pages will be noindex, followed by default, so they will never show up in search results.

Search pages

Title template:

> You searched for %%searchphrase%% on %%sitename%%

404 pages

Title template:

> Page Not Found on %%sitename%%

OK, that's the Titles & Metas sorted out. Let's look at the next set of options.

22.2. Social Settings

To access the 'Social Settings' tabs, click on the '**Social**' link in the SEO menu located left of the WP Dashboard.

These tabs help you to connect your site to Facebook, Twitter & Google+.

Facebook's Open Graph is used by a lot of search engines and social websites to tell them information about your site and about the pages they are visiting.

On the Facebook tab, check the box at the top to '**Add Open Graph Data**'.

With this checked, the plugin will add Facebook Open Graph Meta Tags to your pages:

```
9  <!-- This site is optimized with the Yoast WordPress SEO plugin v1.4.13 -
   http://yoast.com/wordpress/seo/ -->
10 <link rel="canonical" href="http://                    ." />
11 <meta property='og:locale' content='en_US'/>
12 <meta property='og:type' content='website'/>
13 <meta property='og:title' content=                              '/>
14 <meta property='og:url' content='                              '/>
15 <meta property='og:site_name' content=                  />
16 <!-- / Yoast WordPress SEO plugin. -->
17
```

What you do next depends on how you have your Facebook set up. Personally, I have a Facebook 'page' for each of my websites, and I recommend you do the same. You can then '**Add a Facebook Admin**' by clicking the button, and following the instructions on screen. Once you have connected your site to your Facebook profile, you can then add the Facebook Page URL in the settings. This will link the content on your site to your Facebook page.

In the code on your site, you will now see some extra Meta Data added if you check the source code:

```
<meta property='og:locale' content='en_US'/>
<meta property='og:type' content='article'/>
<meta property='og:title' content='                                                      
<meta property='og:description' content=                                                      
                                            '/>
<meta property='og:url' content='http://                              '/>
<meta property='og:site_name' content='                  '/>
<meta property='article:author' content='https://www.facebook.com/          />
<meta property='article:publisher' content='https://www.facebook.com/            '/>
<meta property='fb:admins' content='          2'/>
<meta property='og:image' content='http://                  .com/wp-content/uploads/2012/05/beer-yeast-xs.jpg'/>
<meta property='og:image' content='http://                  .com/images/a80e02dee816_9E41/beer-yeast-xs.jpg'/>
<meta property='og:image' content='http://                  .com/images/a80e02dee816_9E41/peanuts-xs.jpg'/>
<meta property='og:image' content='http://                  .com/images/a80e02dee816_9E41/rice-xs.jpg'/>
```

Notice that there are article:author and article:publisher properties that connects the author to the Facebook page. There are also OpenGraph data elements that specify the images on your page. Now if someone shares your posts on Facebook, these images become available to that person to include next to their post.

OK, that's all we are doing on the Facebook tab. Let's move over to the Twitter tab.

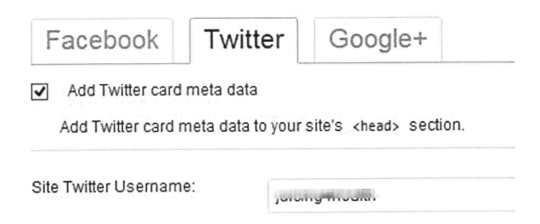

Check the box to add the Twitter card Meta Data to your posts, and enter your Twitter username below.

This will add the following Twitter card data to the source code of your site:

```
<meta name="twitter:card" content="summary"/>
<meta name="twitter:site" content="@j                    "/>
<meta name="twitter:domain" content="J          J          "/>
<meta name="twitter:creator" content="@                    "/>
<meta name="twitter:image:src" content="http://              .com/wp-content/uploads/2012/05/beer-yeast-xs.jpg"/>
<meta name="twitter:image:src" content="http://              .com/images/a80e02dee816_9E41/beer-yeast-xs.jpg"/>
<meta name="twitter:image:src" content="http://              .com/images/a80e02dee816_9E41/peanuts-xs.jpg"/>
<meta name="twitter:image:src" content="http://              .com/images/a80e02dee816_9E41/rice-xs.jpg"/>
```

When anyone tweets with a link to your site, the tweet will contain the usual stuff, but Twitter also scrapes the card data. When viewing the Tweet, the default view is the summary of the tweet (140 characters), but that can now be expanded to show the full Twitter card data.

For more information on Twitter cards, I suggest you read this post on the Twitter website:

https://dev.twitter.com/docs/cards

Finally we have the Google + settings.

First of all, select the author of the homepage (usually yourself), from the dropdown box at the top. This ensures that you will be assigned the author in the source code, using the all-important rel="author" property.

The box underneath is only to be used if you have setup a business page on Google Plus for your website. If you have one, add the URL of the page here, and that page will be assigned as the publisher of the content on the site.

22.3. XML Sitemap Settings

From the SEO menu on the left of the WP Dashboard, select 'XML Sitemaps'. Having an XML sitemap for your site is really important. While it's not much use to visitors, it's a big help to search engines, as they use it to find your site's content.

Incidentally, with good navigation on your site, a search box, and a well-designed homepage, your visitors should not need a sitemap in order to find your content!

On the SEO -> XML sitemaps settings, check the box at the top to enable XML sitemaps. The screen will then expand to show more options.

Under the 'User sitemap' section, check the box for 'Disable author/user sitemap'.

Under 'General settings', I enable the pings to Yahoo and Ask.com, so that these search engines are also informed (Google is automatically informed), when new content is posted on the site.

Under the 'Exclude post types', I have pages and media checked, so no sitemaps are generated for these types. The only post types I want included in my sitemap are the post articles, and if you setup your site the way I do in this book, you will too.

Under the 'Exclude taxonomies', I check the Format box only. However, I setup my 'Category pages' and 'Tag pages', to show an introduction, followed by excerpts of all posts in that group. If you set up your category and tag pages the way I do, leave those boxes unchecked. If you have your category & tag pages set as default (without an introduction), then check those boxes too.

Under the 'Entries per page', you have the option of limiting a sitemap to a certain number of entries. If you leave this blank, the plugin defaults to 1000. Since Google can read sitemaps with 10s of thousands of entries, I leave this box blank, and suggest you do too.

When you have finished, click the 'Save Settings' button.

You can now grab the URL(s) of your sitemap(s), and submit them to Google. You can find the sitemap by clicking the button at the top:

This opens the sitemap in your default web browser.

22.3.1. Submitting Your Sitemap(s) to Google

Earlier in the book, I recommended you sign up for Google Webmaster Tools (GWT). One of the reasons was to submit your sitemap(s) to Google, so that your site would be spidered and indexed quicker. By submitting your sitemap to Google, you are telling them directly that these are the important URLs for them to consider.

The first step is to login to GWT, and select the site you are working on. Then, in the side menu, go to **Crawl -> Sitemaps.**

In the top right of the sitemaps screen, you'll see a button to **Add/Test Sitemap.** Click it now.

Complete the URL of your sitemap, and then click on the '**Submit Sitemap**' button.

NOTE: If you prefer, you can click the '**Test Sitemap**' button first to make sure you are using the correct URL, and that Google can crawl the sitemap properly. If you do that, just repeat the steps above to submit it once you are sure your sitemap status is okay.

Your newly submitted sitemap will be shown as pending. It usually takes a minute or two for Google to visit the sitemap and report back, so just wait a couple of minutes, and then refresh your browser. You should then see confirmation that Google spidered your sitemap and found the pages/images:

NOTE: If you have the '**Google XML Sitemap for Videos**' plugin installed, you can also submit your video sitemap in the same way.

22.4. Permalinks Settings

From the SEO menu on the left of the WP Dashboard, select '**Permalinks**'. These are basically the URLs of your pages as defined in the Settings -> Permalinks section of the Dashboard. We set those up earlier. However, the Yoast plugin gives us a few more options.

Remember when we setup the permalinks, I told you that category page URLs included the word 'category' in them? We had the opportunity to change that word to anything we chose, by entering a 'category base word'. Well Yoast's plugin allows you to remove the word 'category' altogether from all the category pages.

This is the first option on the '**Permalink Settings**' screen.

Personally, I leave it unchecked because I think the word 'category' helps both the search engines and site visitors, to know exactly where they are.

The second option of adding a trailing slash is also not needed, so leave that unchecked too.

The next option, '**Redirect attachment URLs to parent post URL**' is a good idea, so check that. When you upload a media file, WordPress creates an attachment file for the media, which can appear in the search engines. This option redirects these attachment files to the post the media was attached to instead.

The next two options, '**Remove the ?replytocom variables**', and '**Redirect ugly URLs..**' can both be left unchecked.

The final option on the permalinks screen is the '**Canonical Settings**'. This can be left as '**Leave default**'.

22.5. Internal Links Settings

From the SEO menu on the left of the WP Dashboard, select '**Internal Links**'. These options allow you to use breadcrumbs on your site. This is the navigation at the top of the post which shows a link to the home page, one to the category of the post, and the post name. They are designed to help visitors understand exactly where they are on your site.

I actually recommend you leave these settings blank, and just use the breadcrumb navigation that your theme is likely to have built into it.

22.6. RSS Settings

From the SEO menu on the left of the WP Dashboard, select 'RSS'. The settings of the RSS screen are very useful and can help us combat spammers (the people who scrape our content using our RSS feeds, and then post it on their own sites). We can insert special text into the RSS feed, before, and/or after each item in the feed.

Yoast has set the default message as:

This text will be inserted after each item in the feed, with the variable **%%POSTLINK%%** replaced by a hyperlink to the post, using the post title as anchor text, and **%%BLOGLINK%%** replaced by a hyperlink using the name of our site as the anchor text.

Now, if any internet bot scrapes an article from the site and posts it on another site, this code will be inserted into that post, providing links to the original site. This can potentially help Google identify the original author (along with the Google authorship which we set up), so I would leave these settings at their default, with this code inserted into the '**Content to put after each post**' box.

22.7. Import & Export Settings

We can ignore these as they are used to import SEO settings from other popular SEO plugins.

22.8. Edit Files Settings

If you ever need to quickly edit your .htaccess file, you can do so here, as long as it is writable on your server. This is not something we need to do now though.

OK, those are the SEO settings for Yoast's excellent WordPress SEO plugin. This plugin gives us tremendous power and control over the 'SEO settings' for our site, and the content it hosts.

The final part of this book shows how to setup another very important SEO plugin called 'W3 Total Cache'. It helps to speed up the load times of your website, so is very useful. Let's take a closer look.

23. W3 Total Cache Setup

W3 Total Cache is one of two very good WordPress caching plugins. The other is WP Super Cache. If you are a WordPress veteran, and have always used, and are happy with WP Super Cache, then I suggest you continue to use it.

If you have used W3 Total Cache before and know how to set it up for your server, then simply ignore this section.

Setting up W3 Total cache can be a little hit and miss sometimes, with some servers (or scripts on pages), disliking specific things you try to enable. It is therefore imperative that you make a backup of your database before you start to set up this plugin. For free, efficient backups, I recommend the '**WP-DB Manager**' plugin, mentioned earlier in the plugins section of this book.

I won't be covering all of the settings of this plugin. I will set you up with a good basic configuration though, and one which should be compatible with most servers, templates, plugins and scripts. However, if you find your site has any problem loading, simply reverse the changes you made, or deactivate the plugin altogether.

OK, so before we look at how to setup this plugin, let's just cover the why again. Here are a couple of reasons *why* a caching plugin is a good idea.

1. In terms of SEO, the faster the site loads the better.
2. In terms of your visitor, no one likes to hang around waiting for your web page loads. If it takes too long (we're talking in seconds here), then they'll be hitting the back button and checking out your competitor sites instead.

23.1. Setting up W3 Total Cache

I will assume you have already installed and activated the plugin, since we covered that earlier.

In your WordPress Dashboard (left side column), you have a new set of items under the '**Performance**' menu.

NOTE: I won't cover all of these settings, so just change the ones I do mention to the appropriate values. Assume that all other settings can be left at their default values.

23.1.1. General Settings

Click on the 'General Settings' menu item.

This is where we can toggle the various caches on or off. Once they are toggled on, we go to another area of the settings to configure each of the caches.

Page Cache:

1. Enable page cache.
2. Page cache method – Disk enhanced.

Minify:

1. Enable minify.
2. Minify mode set to auto.
3. Minify cache method – Disk.
4. HTML minifier – Default
5. JS Minifier – JSMin (default)
6. CSS minifier – Default

Database Cache:

1. Enable database cache.
2. Database Cache Method – Disk

Object Cache:

1. Enable object cache.
2. Object cache method – Disk.

Browser cache:

1. Enable browser cache.

CDN:

Leave disabled for now. This is something you can activate and setup later, but you should contact your host support first, as some hosts, like StableHost, have easy integration with CDN, and it made a big difference to the stability of my site.

All other settings on the General Settings menu can be left at their default values.

Make sure you click the '**Save all settings**' button before moving on.

Return now to the '**Performance**' menu on the left of the WP Dashboard. You need to select each of the following items it in turn, and configure their settings as follows:

23.1.2. Page Cache
General:

1. Enable 'Cache front page'.
2. Enable 'Cache feeds: site, categories, tags, comments'.
3. Enable 'Cache requests only for mydomain.com site address'.
4. Enable 'Don't cache pages for logged in users'.

Leave all other settings in the Page Cache at their default settings.

23.1.3. Minify
General:

1. Enable 'Rewrite URL structure'.
2. Set 'Minify error notification' to Admin Notification.

HTML & XML:

1. Enable HTML minify settings.
2. Check Inline CSS minification.
3. Check inline JS minification.
4. Check line break removal.

23.1.4. Browser Cache

General:

1. Enable 'Set last-modified header'.
2. Enable 'Set expires header'.
3. Enable 'Set cache control header'.
4. Set 'Entity tag (eTag)'.
5. Set 'W3 Total Cache header'.
6. Enable 'HTTP (gzip compression)'.

That's it! Your W3 Total Cache is now configured with conservative settings.

Now go back to the '**Performance**' menu on the left of the WP Dashboard, and click on the button at the top to '**empty all caches**'.

Now head on over to GTMetrix.com and check your homepage speed. After the first check, hit the back button and check it a second time. The first time will take longer, but now the page is cached, so the second run will give you a better idea of your true page load time.

Here is one of my pages **BEFORE** installing W3 Total Cache:

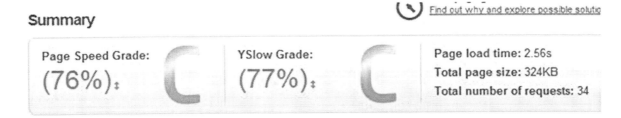

And here is the same page **AFTER** W3 cache was installed and configured (these are the results on the second run after clearing the cache):

Summary

Page Speed Grade: (92%)↑	**A**	YSlow Grade: (90%)↑	**A**	Page load time: 0.82s Total page size: 250KB Total number of requests: 26

NOTE: I found a problem running '**VIA Curation**' plugin on one of my sites with W3 Total cache activated. The submission form would fail to render sometimes. The solution was to exclude the submission form page from W3 Total Cache.

You'll see a box in the Page Cache section. To find it go to Performance -> Page Cache -> Advanced -> Never cache the following pages:

Never cache the following pages:

```
wp-.*\php
index\php
/visitor-recipes/
```

Just enter the slug of the page (page filename), into the box. There may already be items in there, so just add your page(s) at the end.

Useful resources

All resources mentioned in this book can be found here:

http://ezseonews.com/wpseo

Please leave a review on Amazon

If you enjoyed this book, or even if you didn't, I'd love to hear your comments about it. You can leave your thoughts on the Amazon website.

Search Amazon for **B00ECF70HU**

My other Kindle books

Wordpress For Beginners

Do you want to build a website but scared it's too difficult?

Building a website was once the domain of computer geeks. Not anymore. WordPress makes it possible for anyone to create and run a professional looking website

While WordPress is an amazing tool, the truth is it does have a steep learning curve, even if you have built websites before using different tools. Therefore, the goal of this book is to take anyone, even a complete beginner, and get them building a professional looking website. I'll hold your hand, step-by-step, all the way.

As I was planning this book, I made one decision early on. I wanted to use screenshots of everything so that the reader wasn't left looking for something on their screen that I was describing in text. This book has plenty of screenshots. I haven't counted them all, but it must be close to 300. These images will help you find the things I am talking about. They'll help you check your settings and options against the screenshot of mine. You look, compare, and move on to the next section.

With so many screenshots, you may be concerned that the text might be a little on the skimpy side. No need to worry there. I have described every step of your journey in great detail. In all, this publication has over 35,000 words.

This book will surely cut your learning curve associated with WordPress.

Every chapter of the book ends with a "Tasks to Complete" section. By completing these tasks, you'll not only become proficient at using WordPress, but you'll become confident & enjoy using it too.

Search Amazon for **B009ZVO3H6**

SEO 2013 & Beyond

Search Engine Optimization will Never be the Same Again!

 On February 11th, 2011, Google dropped a bombshell on the SEO community when they released the Panda update. Panda was designed to remove low quality content from the search engine results pages. The surprise to many webmasters were some of the big name casualties that got taken out by the update.

On 24th April 2012, Google went in for the kill when they released the Penguin update. Few SEOs that had been in the business for any length of time could believe the carnage that this update caused. If Google's Panda was a 1 on the Richter scale of updates, Penguin was surely a 10. It completely changed the way we needed to think about SEO.

On September 28th 2012, Google released a new algorithm update targeting exact match domains (EMDs). I have updated this book to let you know the consequences of owning EMDs, and added my own advice on choosing domain names. While I have never been a huge fan of exact match domains anyway, many other SEO books and courses teach you to use them. I'll tell you why I think those other courses and books are wrong. The EMD update was sandwiched in between another Panda update (on the 27th September) and another Penguin update (5th October).

Whereas Panda seems to penalize low quality content, Penguin is more concerned about overly aggressive SEO tactics. The stuff that SEOs had been doing for years, not only didn't work anymore, but could now actually cause your site to be penalized and drop out of the rankings. That's right, just about everything you have been taught about Search Engine Optimization in the last 10 years can be thrown out the Window. Google have moved the goal posts.

I have been working in SEO for around 10 years at the time of writing, and have always tried to stay within the guidelines laid down by Google. This has not always been easy because to compete with other sites, it often meant using techniques that Google frowned upon. Now, if you use those techniques, Google is likely to catch up with you and demote your rankings. In this book, I want to share with you the new SEO. **The SEO for 2013 and Beyond.**

Search Amazon for **B0099RKXE8**

An SEO Checklist

A step-by-step plan for fixing SEO problems with your web site

A step-by-step plan for fixing SEO problems with your web site

Pre-Panda and pre-Penguin, Google tolerated certain activities. Post-Panda and post-Penguin, they don't. As a result, they are now enforcing their Webmaster Guidelines which is something that SEOs never really believed Google would do! Essentially, Google have become far less tolerant of activities that they see as rank manipulation.

As webmasters, we have been given a choice. Stick to Google's rules, or lose out on free traffic from the world's biggest search engine.

Those that had abused the rules in the past got a massive shock. Their website(s), which may have been at the top of Google for several years, dropped like a stone. Rankings gone, literally overnight!

To have any chance of recovery, you MUST clean up that site. However, for most people, trying to untangle the SEO mess that was built up over several years is not always easy. Where do you start?

That's why this book was written. It provides a step-by-step plan to fix a broken site. This book contains detailed checklists plus an explanation of why those things are so important.

The checklists in this book are based on the SEO that I use on a daily basis. It's the SEO I teach my students, and it's the SEO that I know works. For those that embrace the recent changes, SEO has actually become easier as we no longer have to battle against other sites whose SEO was done 24/7 by an automated tool or an army of cheap labor. Those sites have largely been removed, and that has leveled the playing field.

If you have a site that lost its rankings, this book gives you a step-by-step plan and checklist to fix problems that are common causes of ranking penalties.

Search Amazon for **B00BXFAULK**

Kindle Publishing

Format, Publish & Promote your books on Kindle

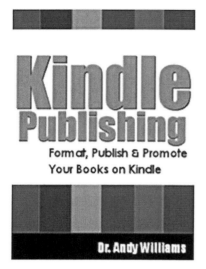

Why Publish on Amazon Kindle?

Kindle publishing has captured the imagination of aspiring writers. Now, more than at any other time in our history, an opportunity is knocking. Getting your books published no longer means sending out hundreds of letters to publishers and agents. It no longer means getting hundreds of rejection letters back. Today, you can write and publish your own books on Amazon Kindle without an agent or publisher.

Is it Really Possible to Make a Good Income as an Indie Author?

The fact that you are reading this book description tells me you are interested in publishing your own material on Kindle. You may have been lured here by promises of quick riches. Well, I have good news and bad. The bad news is that publishing and profiting from Kindle takes work and dedication. Don't just expect to throw up sub-par material and make a killing in sales. You need to produce good stuff to be successful at this. The good news is that you can make a very decent living from writing and publishing on Kindle.

My own success with Kindle Publishing

As I explain at the beginning of this book, I published my first Kindle book in August 2012, yet by December 2012, just 5 months later, I was making what many people consider being a full time income. As part of my own learning experience, I setup a Facebook page in July 2012 to share my Kindle publishing journey (there is a link to the Facebook page inside this book). On that Facebook page, I shared the details of what I did, and problems I needed to overcome. I also shared my growing income reports, and most of all, I offered help to those who asked for it. What I found was a huge and growing audience for this type of education, and ultimately, that's why I wrote this book.

What's in this Book?

This book covers what I have learned on my journey and what has worked for me. I have included sections to answer the questions I myself asked, as well as those questions people asked me. This book is a complete reference manual for successfully formatting, publishing & promoting your books on Amazon Kindle. There is even a section for non-US publishers because there is stuff there you specifically need to know. I see enormous potential in Kindle Publishing, and in 2013 I intend to grow this side of my own business. Kindle publishing has been liberating for me and I am sure it will be for you too.

Search Amazon for **B00BEIX34C**

CSS for Beginners

Learn CSS with detailed instructions, step-by-step screenshots and video tutorials showing CSS in action on real sites

Most websites and blogs you visit use cascading style sheets (CSS) for everything from fonts selection & formatting, to layout & design. Whether you are building WordPress sites or traditional HTML websites, this book aims to take the complete beginner to a level where they are comfortable digging into the CSS code and making changes to their own site. This book will show you how to make formatting & layout changes to your own projects quickly and easily.

The book covers the following topics:

- Why CSS is important
- Classes, Pseudo Classes, Pseudo Elements & IDs
- The Float property
- Units of Length
- Using DIVs
- Tableless Layouts, including how to create 2-column and 3-column layouts
- The Box Model
- Creating Menus with CSS
- Images & background images

The hands on approach of this book will get YOU building your own Style Sheets from scratch. Also included in this book:

- Over 160 screenshots and 20,000 words detailing ever step you need to take.
- Full source code for all examples shown.
- Video Tutorials.

The video tutorials accompanying this book show you:

- How to investigate the HTML & CSS behind any website.

- How to experiment with your own design in real time, and only make the changes permanent on your site when you are ready.

A basic knowledge of HTML is recommended, although all source code from the book can be downloaded and used as you work through the book.

Search Amazon for **B00AFV44NS**

More information from Dr. Andy Williams

If you would like more information, tips, tutorials or advice, there are two resources you might like to consider.

The first is my free weekly newsletter over at ezSEONews.com offering tips, tutorials and advice to online marketers and webmasters. Just sign up and my newsletter, plus SEO articles, will be delivered to your inbox. I cannot always promise a weekly schedule, but I do try ;)

I also run a course over at CreatingFatContent.com, where I build real websites in front of members in "real-time" using my system of SEO.

11703504R00092

Printed in Great Britain
by Amazon.co.uk, Ltd.,
Marston Gate.